Legacy

Loops

a memoir

Healing Me, Healing You

Sherri A. Lynn

Legacy Loops
a memoir
Healing Me, Healing You

This work depicts actual events in the life of the author as truthfully as recollection permits and/or can be verified by research. Occasionally, dialogue consistent with the character or nature of the person speaking has been supplemented. All persons within are actual individuals; there are no composite characters. The names of some individuals have been changed to respect their privacy.

Published by
Sherri A. Lynn
New Jersey

Cover design: Eric Labacz, labaczdesign.com
Rear Cover Photo Credits: Sherri & Goat – Marie Acacia
Sherri in Tree Pose – Valerie McConnell

To the Silently Suffering
Caught in the Crosshairs of Denial.
May you find your way to peace, healing, and wholeness.

And
To the three J's I miss so deeply.
My favorite part of the day was always spending it with you!

And
To the inner child within.
May you experience far more love than fear.
You are enough.

A Note to Readers:

This book contains themes involving generational abuse, trauma, molestation, addiction, neglect, and more. Please practice self-care when reading this book and know that recovery is possible.

About The Cover

It took a few tries to arrive at a cover that captured the true essence of this book's chapters.

Taken in the late 1970's, the polaroid photo shows me as a young teen shaking paw with my new puppy. Beyond the tear in the photo, my adult profile, contemplative, as I continued writing and healing from childhood.

Upon first seeing the draft, I sobbed. I sobbed for everything that younger version of me lost. And everything I was forced to defend against. Because of recovery, I am able to look at the cover today filled with a sense of pride no one can ever take away. And puppies…who doesn't like looking at pictures of puppies?

Thank you, Eric Labacz, for the mastery in designing another amazing cover.

Contents

Chapter 1

Baking New Memories

Christmas, 2023

It was the first Christmas since 2015 that I didn't cry. I didn't cry waking up. I didn't cry during the day. And I didn't cry going to sleep. I charted a new course and created for myself a really good day.

In 2015, I cried because I was told by my jealous, abusive, older sibling that "we won't be opening presents at my house Christmas day...with dinner and the kids and all, it's just too much chaos and confusion". When I arrived, I saw they prepared lasagna—ahead of time.

Well, that's bullshit. How confusing and chaotic is that? There's more to this story. I'm sure of it.

The house had a weird feel to it. My so-called family felt more avoidant than usual. Either they were hiding something, or I was becoming paranoid. It did not feel like Christmas. The kids, my oldest nibling's offspring, weren't opening gifts. Instead of packages and piles of paper marking the scene of a celebratory unwrapping frenzy, there sat the well-worn hardwood floor covered by an old area rug.

Who does that? Who doesn't WANT to see their grandkids opening a bunch of presents on Christmas Day? Someone who is jealous and resentful.

It didn't take long to get to the bottom of the awkwardness. "Presents" were opened earlier one town over, and I was the only family member not there. I wasn't there because they kept it from me. I thought it had been just the littles and their parents at the gift opening, but when I asked my sibling if they were there, I received the infamous "I one-upped you again" evil grin. I was the only one NOT there. It stung.

Sometime after the lame lasagna, I was invited to do presents and dinner when the in-laws did *their* exchange with the littles. As dinnertime for *that* approached, I was subsequently UNinvited through a cowardly text from my sibling's eldest child—their forty-year-old replica. I became incensed with "the family" and felt terrible for the completely innocent children caught in the crosshairs of dysfunction and sibling jealousy.

Days passed.

I received a snotty, snarky call from the replica. "The kids wanna know when they're going to get their presents from you." (As if it were somehow *my* doing that they had *NOT* received them yet.) "They are welcome at my house any time to retrieve their gifts. As for the rest of you…I've already returned everything. I won't be going through this again." And didn't.

In 2016, I seized an opportunity to give the trio their presents days ahead of Christmas. I reminded them of the events of the previous year. How Aunt Sherri wasn't included in the morning opening of presents and how I missed seeing their excitement. I told them that the Big Man (Santa) really hooked us up this year…and how they must have been extra good to be able to open so many gifts early. It was fantastic! An added bonus was that I didn't have to worry about whether or not I was included in anything. Once the kids left my house that night, I had already decided Christmas was over. When Christmas actually came, I hiked. Spontaneous tears leaked out when I thought of those children and how I hoped they'd be safe without me.

The next six Christmases would also have tears. Some more than others. I didn't realize how much emotional excavation I'd have to do surrounding the holidays. I'd learned that there were so many components, so many levels. I had trauma around cookies, decorating, gift giving, and what I was supposed to do or where I "had to" be at any given moment. The simple fact that I was an adult with the emotional intelligence of a child as it pertained to holidays was a legacy loop that has taken me a very long time to understand, much less commence creating new circuits.

***

I like cookies--especially the everyday varieties like chocolate chip walnut, thin mints, and Chinese almond cookies. Christmas cookies are a bit of a different story. As of 2023, Christmas cookies could still evoke a visceral response in my body. And because in my mind I knew they were "only cookies", I couldn't fully understand why my insides reacted the way they did. It has taken years to recognize the legacy loop and begin to unsugar coat it. My gut also recognizes how the loop spans multiple generations and is tightly enmeshed with dysfunction. There is *nothing* sweet about it!

***

Mom was a holiday baker. She made pies for Thanksgiving and Easter and roasting pans full of cookies to give away at Christmas. Many of the varieties were labor intensive and time consuming. Some required the dough to be made ahead of time and refrigerated; others required the tedious task of unwrapping dozens of Hershey kisses or the shelling, picking, and grinding of nuts. As a youngster, I was commanded to stay out of the kitchen, but eventually, I was allowed to "help" with some of the more menial and harmless pieces of the process.

What started as "fun helping mom" evolved into a deep denial about dysfunction and what those cookies truly represented in my family of origin. My grandmother thoroughly enjoyed my mother's confections. In time, I would see it as one of the very few ways my mother could get *her* mother's love, approval, and acknowledgement…if only for a few brief moments each year. My mother just "being herself" was never enough for my grandmother. I was looped in with an energetic lasso that tightened like a noose with each passing year of baking. At some point, it stopped being fun. It had become an angry holiday chore that *HAD TO GET DONE!* Guilt, anger, and obligation became the binding agents.

After our mother died, my older sibling stepped into our mother's baking shoes, using many of the same labor-intensive recipes. By feigning helplessness, others were hypnotized into helping the master manipulator create *artificially sweetened* Christmas treats—for years. First it was me and my friends; then, the tradition was dumped onto my sibling's kids with the same guilt I received as a child. The cookies expanded into dog treats, and the orders grew. My sibling's energetic cup was filled first by exploiting the goodness of those who helped, then further by the confection recipients through their accolades. It was a vicious cycle. A narcissist's dream. I finally saw it for what it was and stayed clear.

How can I undo the emotional damage I suffered? They're just cookies, right?

***

A dear friend also had emotional pain around a particular type of Christmas cookie. Our situations were similar. We both had become estranged from children we loved dearly through no fault of our own. Their parents enjoyed using their children as chess pieces in a sick dysfunctional game that involved fear and manipulation.

***

Annually, my friend *used* to make sugar cookies with one of her daughters. She's tearfully shared the story with me several times. "It's hard to know if you're making an impression on them sometimes…you know?" I nodded. "We made the cookies together for years." She paused, gathering her thoughts and emotions, still deeply feeling the loss. My friend told of how *before* they became estranged, her daughter recalled one of the times they baked together. "Mama, remember the time when we were making those cookies, and I said there's flour all over…we're making a mess!?" My friend paused again, overcome by recalling the conversation. I sensed that my friend was back in that kitchen with her daughter reliving the moment, a moment that was wonderful confirmation that an impression *had* been made through all those years of baking together. My friend returned to her present-day kitchen with me and finished the story of how her daughter said, "Yes, Mama, and you said, 'No, Sweetie, we're not making a mess; we're making memories.'"

My friend's pain was also mine. We shared an annual emotional pain loop that held us both captive for different reasons. Together, we decided to create a new cookie memory. We planned a day to make those sugar cookies and release ourselves from pain. My friend had *at least* a bazillion toppings and a half a bazillion cookie shapes. One was supposed to be a heart. Truth be told, it looked more like a penis to me—not exactly a fitting tribute for two lesbian bakers. I tried to be respectful, but once I saw it as a pecker, there was really no "unseeing" it that way.

How can we possibly sell that thing as a heart?

Truly?

Fate intervened.

The oven became incensed and parched the peckers. Laughter ensued. It was the kind of laughter that was contagious. Mission accomplished. Unlike the *artificially sweetened* cookies of the master manipulator, this new cookie memory was baked with love. And is it sweet!

Chapter 2

Tree Trauma Tamed

"You *have* to have a Christmas tree!" a former girlfriend proclaimed.

No, I don't.

"Yes, you do!"

No, I really don't.

That girlfriend showed up at my house one day with a handmade ceramic tree with lights that someone in her family made some 400 years earlier or something. A favorite aunt or somebody close. I really can't remember the specific details because the whole tree thing sent my limbic system into overdrive. Back then, I didn't know it was my limbic system firing; I only knew my insides were scrambling for a place to hide—signs of another legacy loop. Through temper-tantrum induced tears, I demanded she pack it back up in the black plastic garbage bag she brought it in and take it back home with her. *I don't want it here!*

***

"Everybody has a Christmas tree," said another woman I dated some years later.

I don't care what everybody else has. I don't need or want a friggin' tree in my house.

I managed to dodge the whole tree thing that year by explaining an old painful memory of how I put up a tree many years earlier to surprise a live-in girlfriend. It wasn't *my* thing, but it was *hers*. The relationship had lost its spark, and I tried using the tree to re-ignite it. It didn't work.

***

It's just a tree...right? I've got to try and get to the bottom of this tree thing. Clear up some of the emotion and bad memories around it somehow. Maybe I'll try tapping.

***

Many years ago, one of my therapists guided me through how to use tapping for pain and limiting beliefs about myself. I was in such a state back then that I would have tried just about anything for relief. I remember thinking how strange it looked and felt doing. But I also knew I grew to trust this therapist and how much better I felt afterward. There was no denying the results *this* skeptic experienced. Today, there are countless videos on the Internet on how to use it for practically everything.

***

Tapping, also known as EFT or Emotional Freedom Technique, was created by Gary Craig in the 1990's. According to the Newport Institute's website (www.newportinstitute.com), *...like acupuncture and acupressure, it utilizes points along the body's energy meridians—the "highways" or channels through which the body's energy flows, according to Chinese medicine.*

"Often with specific anxiety, the patients are aware of the events or memories that trigger the discomfort. Using EFT, the patient revisits the event(s) in question, the energy meridians are thus re-disturbed, and then the physical symptoms caused by that particular disturbance can be healed by correcting the meridians with EFT." (EFT founder Gary Craig)

***

I was ready to do some healing work around my *adult* Christmas tree trauma. After several deep cleansing breaths, I had reached a place of peace and was ready to start the process. Brad Yates' instructional videos explain that he is NOT a doctor and start with disclaimers and about "taking responsibility for your own well-being". I began tapping on the first point. With the first three fingers of my right hand, I gently tapped the outside edge of my left hand, just below the base of the pinky. I spoke the tree issue aloud three times before moving to the second tapping point. *Even though I have this emotional pain around putting up a Christmas tree, I deeply love and approve of myself.* As I moved through the different tapping points and continued speaking aloud, I could feel something in my gut stirring. *Holy Holly tree, it's working!* It only took a few moments before I realized I had to puke...right now! I ran to the bathroom and did just that. I puked before even finishing a complete cycle of tapping all the points!

* * *

WHOA! THAT was some deep-seated stuff, and it was definitely ready to be released!

After I checked in with myself, I discovered that I felt good enough to put up the Christmas tree that year and did. It felt good to reclaim a part of myself that I had lost to others' traditions and beliefs. I *chose* to put up a tree for myself and did. I felt like I had finally neutralized the neurons around everyone else's Nativity normal. Soon after the holiday, I donated that tree to The Raptor Trust in Millington, NJ. The owls there loved it!

If I decide to have a tree again in the future, I can just go out and get another one. For now, I'm content with being done with them.

I successfully managed to waltz around the Christmas tree trauma for several more years before the loop snared me again. This time, with much of the emotion dispersed, I could state my needs like an adult instead of a cranky child. The woman I had been dating for about five months *loved* the holidays, especially Christmas. That particular year, she wanted to check an item off her bucket list and cut down her own tree. We had had a few discussions around the holidays, and she was content not to push me. She was so excited about the visit to the tree farm that it was contagious. *Listen, I want to support you with your bucket list item...here's what I can do. I'd like to take the ride with you to the tree place and help with the process. Once we have the tree in the stand, the rest is up to you. I'm outta here. That work?* Smiling wide, she nodded in agreement. I came to learn that what I actually did that day was set and execute a healthy boundary. It felt amazing.

Almost immediately, we found a perfectly-shaped tree, but it was too small for the space she had chosen. We walked around until my girlfriend spotted "the one.". I took plenty of pictures as her bucket list item commenced. Once complete, we returned to the site of the small tree. *Hey, why not get this one too...for your patio outside?* She agreed. And *I* got to cut that one down myself! It was fun, especially since it wasn't going to *my* house, and *I* didn't have to decorate it!

We returned to her house and secured the trees in their stands. I left feeling pretty good about how the whole thing unfolded. No upset stomach, anxiety, *or* puking! Tree trauma tamed. And that's healing!

Chapter 3
Legacy Layers

"It's like peeling the layers of an onion." They say.
Well, how fucking big is the onion? I wanna know!

***

It was sometime before Christmas, 2023. With more than a year of recovery in Adult Children of Alcoholics (ACA), I was learning to say "no" without feeling fiercely compelled to explain or defend myself. I was unapologetically making choices that felt right, safe, and good for me. It was getting easier to take care of my own wants and needs without feeling guilty. It sure felt different! I made the decision to keep presents and parties to a bare minimum. Finding myself single for over a year helped—just knowing I wouldn't feel pressured to put on the fake holiday face took some of the usual Christmas edge off.

I accepted a friend's invitation for lunch and a splash in her hot tub. It was an easy decision since my body had been feeling achy, and she's also a really good cook. She has a comfortable, welcoming home on a small lake about 20 minutes from me. I walked inside, left my shoes at the door, and greeted her cats like I always do.

As I rounded the corner into the living room, my body was forced to stop. It felt as if there were an invisible forcefield keeping me from advancing any further. Before me stood a beautifully-shaped Christmas tree. Perfectly decorated. Beneath its branches were dozens of perfectly-placed packages wrapped with love.

It's just a tree, Sherri. It's just a tree. Isn't it gorgeous?

After what felt like forever, I realized I wasn't breathing. I had to force myself to take a breath. And did. As I started to snap out of it, my friend asked if I could do her a favor and water it. Having recently had one knee replaced and scheduled for the other, she wasn't exactly in the position of getting down on either of her knees just yet.

The needles brushed my cheeks as I reached in with the water pitcher. Their piney scent both tickled and tortured my senses and sensibility. Legacy loops were strangling my memories and emotions. Moments later, sticky sap on my fingertips brought on the tears. The tears of an unexpected breakup and a bucket-list tree memory that were tangled like discarded holiday string lights.

I rose to my feet and found my way to the nearest chair. And cried.

It's just a tree, right? It's just a fucking tree! I said to my friend through clouded eyes.

Have I lost my mind? It's just a tree. It's beautiful too. My eyes can see that. Where is this coming from, and when will it stop?

My friend was gracious, loving, kind, patient, and understanding. She held an energetic healing space as I worked through my thoughts, memories, and emotions around the tree. Turns out I have a lot of repressed and unexpressed emotions surrounding Christmas trees—and not just the adult ones I thought I had already dealt with.

***

Growing up, *our* house had a fake tree while my maternal grandmother *always* had to have a live tree. Mom defended her choice; Gramma defended hers. Silently, through threatening looks and body language, I felt each of them wanted me to side with them. I found myself in an awkward position. I was just a kid and was caught in a tug of war between two women who acted like two gnarly dogs on opposite ends of a knotted rope toy. Looking back, I hated those moments and the feelings they stirred inside of me.

How the tree was decorated was also a source of contention. Gramma had to use gaudy garland, and mom tinsel that came in small boxes. I don't remember it being a simple difference of opinion. I remember it as an angry act of defiance. *It's just a tree...right?*

***

I have so many unsettling memories around Christmas-tree decorating. I remember the super fragile glass ornaments my family had before my parents split; some were perfectly round, and some were oblong-ish with a point on the bottom and an indented circle in the middle that was adorned with glitter. They were beyond delicate and had to be handled with extreme care. I was repeatedly reminded to be careful and pay attention to what I was doing. Truthfully, I was a nervous wreck just being in the same room with the *boxed* ornaments! God forbid I actually broke one!

***

When I close my eyes, I can still hear how unforgiving the hardwood floor was to the ornament that slowly slid off its hanging hook. I can still see the shattered shards of colored glass that scattered everywhere when it exploded on impact. Silent and small Sherri, standing still, solo, holding the tiny piece of wire that once held the ornament…My memory replays it over and over, in slow motion. Before the beating and yelling even started, the familiar taste of salty tears landed on my lips. My feet were frozen in position near the fake Frasier fir as my body shook in anticipation of what was coming. I was in big trouble. My mother didn't rush over to comfort me or check to make sure I was ok. There was none of that. What I actually got was deplorable. As I recall the memory, I can still feel the way my face tingled from how hard I was repeatedly hit that day.

It's just an ornament…Isn't it?

Those legacy layers around tree memories were not sweet like a multi-tiered cake. They were more an invisible choke collar growing tighter with every step I took away from how things were *supposed* to be. I've learned that's exactly how dysfunction works. For me, that "fucking onion" is bringing far fewer tears and shrinks every single day I work my ACA program.

Chapter 4
Gift Giving Angst

"You get what you get, and you like it…no matter what. And you'd better say 'thank you,' or you're gonna get it when we get home! Don't you *dare* embarrass me!"

My mother's threatening words shook my younger self to the core. Tuning in to the memory fifty-something years later can still send my nervous system into overdrive. This particular memory starts my gift-giving angst…and sadly, *still* causes me to get uneasy with certain people. That sensation was looped into my neural network when I was incredibly young. The event and internal bodily reactions that surface are about as hard to forget as the ABC's. It bears mentioning that as of this writing, Mom's been dead almost 40 years.

***

"Here, open this one," the woman I knew as Aunt Jean said as she handed me a small, neatly wrapped package. Even though the package was square, it wasn't much larger than a golf ball.

You'd better like it…no matter what!

I was far from excited opening the package. The fear and panic of not responding the right way robbed any excitement I *might* have had.

Slowly, while rehearsing appropriate appreciation in my head, I removed the gift wrap to reveal a small plastic box. "Oh my God! I LOVE it! Thank you! Thank you SO much!" I said.

What the heck is it? What am I even supposed to do with it? I feel so stupid. This is stupid. A plastic box?

Laughter erupted. My mother and aunt spontaneously laughed at me. The awkwardness I felt standing between them in my aunt's kitchen is still fresh in my body. I had no idea what was so funny. Their reaction made me feel small. Insignificant even. I hung my head low while wishing the speckled-tile kitchen floor would just swallow me up like a sink hole.

"Open it," one of them said.

Huh?

Clearly annoyed I wasn't moving fast enough, one of them yanked the tiny box out of my hand. "Just give it to me...I'll show you."

I remember feeling even more stupid that I didn't know how to open it. They mocked me for not knowing. Once opened, the box revealed the ugliest thing I'd ever seen. It was a gold ring with a square green stone—like something you'd see at an estate sale. Who gives dead-person jewelry to a little kid? *AND* expects them to be overjoyed by it? I'm sure my sad face and droopy body language told the truth about how I *really* felt about this unwanted gift. I hated green and didn't wear jewelry. It was appreciated about as much as the nasty, itchy, ruffly underwear and socks I was UNlovingly "gifted" and forced into as a toddler.

Some gift this is. It feels more like a punishment! The unopened box made me happier.

"Try it on!"

Please don't fit. Please don't fit.

"It's too big. I'm going to put it back in the box so I don't lose it." And lose it I did!

***

The ring thing was strung into my brain's circuitry like plastic beads masquerading as expensive pearls. There were other thoughtless gifts too. Ugly clothes that I wouldn't want to be caught dead in. Even *if* the receipt were included, I was forbidden to exchange whatever it was lest I *hurt so-and-so's feelings. They picked it out special for you!* It felt like torture. I was forcibly forbidden to have my own likes and dislikes.

Once old enough, I did get games and eventually, a ten-speed bike. The games were multiple-player games and never opened. They were put in a larger box and eventually moved around from home to home as I moved. I guess I always secretly hoped someone would show up to play the games with me—they never did. I opened that over-sized carton of unopened games a few years ago looking for something else. I cried. And when I was done crying, I put that box into my car and donated it to

Goodwill. I had held onto that pain long enough. And the bike? It was a piece of crap—the brakes squeaked, and it never did shift into all ten gears.

You get what you get, and you like it…no matter what.

***

Through the years, there were plenty more incidents of agita and angst around the giving and receiving of gifts. Mostly with family members, but some with friends as well. *Did I spend enough? Is it the right size, color, or style? Do they really like it?* Many times, I suffered the same anxiety I did as a kid waiting to see the receiver's *real* reaction to what I gave them.

This is one of the reasons why I avoid attending big parties and showers where attendees watch the celebrant open their gifts. It's also why I'd prefer to *do* something with someone rather than *get* something. I've learned that if I want something, it's best for me to just go get it myself…not to wait on somebody else to come through for me.

Uneasy doesn't adequately describe my gift-giving angst. I've also taken the time to give some really thoughtful gifts and received crappy presents in return. One Christmas, I received a squatty potty poop stool as my "big gift." That's pretty shitty considering the college graduation gift they received from me filled *their* lifelong dream—a trip to Hawaii.

Being estranged from my family of origin has yielded healthy perks. It's allowed me the space to process the anxiety I've had regarding the giving and receiving of gifts. It has also loosened the strangling grip of the legacy loop that kept me on a short leash. I give generously when moved to *and* refrain when I'm not. Giving to animal organizations, child advocacy and welfare groups, and veteran and domestic violence non-profits feels good. Those heartfelt contributions have relieved my gift-giving angst *and* given *me* the best gift ever…

Being unapologetically true to myself!

Chapter 5

Guilt, Growth, Motivation & Manipulation

Guilt is one of those emotions that, when kept in check, can be a very powerful internal motivator. *If I choose to eat the cake, I'll run an extra mile or hit the gym an extra day this week...so I don't feel guilty. If I leave work early today, I'll make up for it by shortening my lunch tomorrow...so I don't feel so bad.*

Conversely, when guilt is used externally to make someone *else* feel bad for *their* choice, it is manipulation—plain and simple. If the person doing the guilting is really slick, like my older sibling, they can present their case so well that it has the *appearance* of motivation. "I know you planned to do X on Thursday, but it would be really helpful to me and so-and-so if you did Y for us instead...it would mean sooooo much to us. We have no other options. No one else can do it like you." (Insert head tilt and batting of eyes)

My genetics grabbed the Olympic gold in guilt. I'm fairly certain it was fed through the umbilical cord for generations. I *know* my mother received the guilt gene from her mother, and I suspect her mother got it from hers as well. Only God knows how many legacy loops it lapped. Just hearing, or writing, or thinking about that word gets my internal circuits firing. Truth be told, I could write an entire series on how guilt shaped me—both in the giving *and* receiving.

***

"Uh, we *have* to go to Gramma's" my mother sighed, defeated. The statement came out like the stale air of an inflated balloon that was unknotted and just let go. Her head and eyes were cast down, shoulders hunched. It was a sad moment indeed. I have a very vivid memory of the scene and the dialogue but can't see or remember how old I was. Mom was clearly sad and not angry that day, so it felt safe enough to ask, "Why?"

"Because she's my mother and we *have* to go."

"But wait; I don't understand…why do we *have* to go someplace we don't *want* to go?"

"Because she's my mother."

***

That was the first time I remember questioning why we were doing something we really didn't want to be doing. The response to subsequent similar questions about why we were doing things was shortened to "because I said so" and eventually to just "because." Sometimes the answer was given in an even tone as if describing the weather, and other times my inquiry seemed to evoke deep, unprocessed anger and frustration. On those days, the retort was given through gritted teeth and aggressive body language—like an upset child stomping their foot to demonstrate they mean business.

Eventually, I stopped asking.

***

The approach to Christmas, 2023 was different for me. Something shifted. With more than a year of recovery in Adult Children of Alcoholics, I had access to new tools, healthier people, and an understanding of why I've defaulted to certain feelings and choices for so long. My "have tos" were changing to an internal dialogue of "do I *want* to?" *I get to make my own plans. Where and how do I want to spend the holiday? Who allows me the freedom to choose without trying to make me feel guilty?*

Initially, I had planned to rent a cabin in the woods to commence the process of audio recording my first two books. Those plans didn't come to fruition because of a minor medical issue with one of my cats. I made peace with staying home.

***

On the days leading up to the holiday, I received a number of invitations from friends and acquaintances. The offers were for events before, during, and after Christmas day. I paid close attention to how each event offer felt in my body. Did it feel good? You know, like did the people asking *really* want me to be there, or did I feel like they were obligated to invite me.

How does this invitation make me feel? Do I feel pressured to go there? Do any of the people attending make me feel uncomfortable? How do I want to spend my time? Will I have fun?

And the most important of all questions.

Will I feel loved?

I shared my feelings with some and completely avoided talking with others. The people I dodged were the ones that I perceived as having very little capacity for listening or understanding. It's almost as if they were born with two mouths and one ear instead of the other way around. I find it amusing how the people I have trouble being around today mirror the person I was before.

Fun fact: I'm a recovering interrupter myself.

Listening carefully helped me choose. The most loving and understanding invitations were my motivators. I wanted to take the chance to either rewrite a rotten memory with a really good one or try something completely new. One of the first people to reach out was the friend I lovingly refer to as my 'sperience buddy because we've had a number of *e*xperiences that generally end up with tears of laughter running down our legs.

"Hey, I know you're not into the Christmas thing…and you don't have to come if it doesn't feel good…but I don't want you to feel left out either…no pressure…ok?" my 'sperience buddy started.

Ok.

"I got these gingerbread house kits for the boys…we can do dinner…but only if you want to."

"Hell yeah! I never did that! That's more like a craft thing than a Christmas thing anyway. What can I bring?"

"Your appetite! There's also this holiday party at the Elk's too…for the kids…we go every year…we don't have to stay the whole time either…you're welcome to come…and my parents are asking about you too…NO PRESSURE!"

I helped make gingerbread houses that would have failed a building inspection, decorated ugly sweater cookies that were really, really, ugly, wreaked havoc at the "kids" Christmas party by getting innocent by-standers mixed up in a fake snowball fight, all prior to Christmas. There were other holiday things I attended, but doing things with kids, especially *these* kids, was what my heart needed.

As December 25th approached, I reached out to a friend I hadn't seen in years. We actually met on Christmas in 2016 at a Washington-Crossing-the-Delaware reenactment at a NJ state park of the same name. The weather was set to be nice, and her family's celebration would be complete by then. She was "in."

That morning, I attended an ACA meeting before heading out to Washington's Crossing State Park to meet my friend for the reenactment. I spotted my friend's dog, Pickle, before my friend. This crafty canine orchestrated our meeting seven years earlier*! Seeing him again after all this time was one of the best gifts ever! Especially since it was obvious he remembered me! Few things validate me like a dog leaning their whole body into mine. *Awww, I missed you too P-dog!* It also felt fantastic to reconnect with my human friend.

My heart is full. This feels amazing! This was a really good choice!

Later, I had dinner and celebrated the holiday with my 'sperience buddy's family and her parents. It was complete with more fake snowballs, fun and thoughtful gifts, dinner, and a whole lotta laughter and love. It truly was the best Christmas I'd had in many, many years! No forced obligations. No fake faces. And best of all, no agita either!

***

Wow! I did it! I made it through Christmas without crying! And I actually enjoyed myself! This is how it's supposed to feel! Thank you, God, for putting these earth angels into my path.

***

With a tear-free Christmas behind me, I was riding high. I

was able to circle back around to the non-listeners. One in particular that I said, "Please, no gifts" to, hit a nerve. "I haven't seen you in over a year." I knew it was a while, but *they* were actually keeping track! And it didn't feel good. It felt like I was *required* to meet some invisible expectation of theirs. I've come to understand that *real friends* don't do that. *Real friends* don't keep score. When I heard it, I felt bad. In fact, I felt so bad for how *they* felt, that I didn't even pay attention to how *I* felt. I had this sudden urge to "get them on the calendar" and did.

It was likely they were going to have a gift for me, but I wasn't moved to shop for them, and didn't. They were *not* one of the few I chose to exchange with, and I was comfortable with *my* decision. Once in their company, I could feel myself falling off center. The feeling was familiar. Since we were in a busy restaurant, there was a lot of activity buzzing around that made processing my own thoughts somewhat challenging. I half-heartedly answered questions while staring at the white tablecloth, attempting to regain my sense of self.

I don't like how this feels. Why am I rehashing things I've already talked through with program friends? What am I doing here? How did this happen?

I knew I was in my body, but it certainly didn't feel like it.

What is this familiar feeling?

My *friend* must have sensed something. She reached over, grabbed my chin, and spun my head to face her as she said, "Look at me when you're talking to me." *Nope…that doesn't feel good…that doesn't feel good at all.* I turned back to face the tablecloth like a child that had just been scolded. *You're ok, you're ok. You have choices. You don't have to look at her. She can't force you. Finish your sentence. It's almost time to go.*

The restaurant tables were full and the lobby packed with more hungry diners waiting for a table. Since we were done eating, the servers were nervously pacing nearby giving us silent cues to leave. My insides felt relieved knowing "lunch" was nearly over, and I'd be able to return home to re-center myself. "Want to go somewhere else to finish talking?"

"No thanks, I have to get home. I was already out longer

than I expected to be."

Good job, Sherri! Way to take corrective action and minimize the exposure!

Once outside the restaurant, she handed me a bag with a gift and a sweater we had talked about weeks earlier. I was anxious to get the encounter over with and retreat to the safety of my car and, eventually, my home. My insides were in turmoil, and I recognized I was in childhood survival mode. I don't remember the exact sequence of events, but there were two awkward hugs and the inappropriate tugging of my hoodie hood before we parted. Again, I froze and said nothing.

Why do I do that? Why do I just freeze? What vibe do I give off?

The ride home was a complete blur. I *may* have called someone to talk through the experience. I *may* have just driven home in silence. I really don't remember. I *do* remember I felt floaty, dream-like, and questioned whether it really happened, or if I'd imagined the whole thing. One thing for sure, I was exhausted and fell dead asleep for over two hours!

Upon rising, the gift bag and sweater were sitting in a back bedroom. *Shit! It really happened!*

I was also ready to answer my earlier question. *What is this familiar feeling?*

GUILT! I succumbed to guilt...and she justified it to herself, just like someone else I know! FUCK! I just had an emotional relapse and allowed myself to be manipulated!

*Pickle & Louey's story is in my first book, *All My Heroes Have Fur, Fins & Feathers, An Animal Communicator's Healing Journey of Awakening.*

Chapter 6
Holy Shift

"She did what?"

"She grabbed me by the chin, spun my head around to face her, and said, 'Look at me when you're talking to me'".

"And you didn't clock her? That's just wrong! On so many levels!"

Calmly, another friend explained, "Touch of any kind is an intimate act...to touch someone's face is extremely intimate. That's a serious boundary violation!"

***

Where am I? What day is it?

I woke dazed from the two-hour, midday nap. It was the kind of slumber where you fall fast and hard and completely leave your body and surroundings. I don't know where I went, but I know I was deeply triggered in that restaurant. And now to process it.

Showing up for the guilt lunch tested my nervous system. I recognized something was off with my internals as soon as I arrived. Without immediately knowing exactly what it was, I struggled to regain my balance. My "self" felt fractured. Part of me was in the restaurant, another part of me was someplace else, and yet another part wished I had stayed home. Soldiering on "not to disappoint my friend" increased the intensity of my experience. I did not feel present. It was far too late to realize that *I don't really want to be here!*

Dammit! I did it again. I made a choice I wished I hadn't. Why?

I *know* I come from generations of guilt, fear, and abandonment. I *know* I've likely used that method of getting what I wanted as well. I also *know* I couldn't have done it any other way. It's what was modeled by my caregivers. I *now know* it's neither healthy nor productive. I know better and *want* to do better.

In recovery, it's stated that the solution is "to become my own loving parent.". To do that, I must first forgive myself for attending a lunch out of guilt and not wanting to *abandon* my friend. That's on me. I was the one that gave my power away. The truth is, if I weren't in that person's company, it would have been absolutely impossible for them to put their hands on me *and* shame me into looking at them when I really didn't want to. It's silly to think that by not wanting *them* to feel bad, I actually abandoned myself. No wonder my nervous system was on overload!

Knowing *what* to do, in this case forgiving myself, is progress. Knowing *how* is another story. Forgiving wasn't modeled for me; silence and repressing emotions were…unless the emotion was anger…and *that* was reserved for others. I could *never* be the one to express anger lest I wanted a good beating or mocking.

I remembered an exercise my first therapist taught me. It was a writing exercise. I was to write, "I forgive myself for giving my power away to" and name the person. She suggested I handwrite it out ten times for each person that pulled my strings like a puppet. Looking back, I unknowingly allowed a whole slew of people to take advantage of me. Faithfully, I did the exercise a couple times a day, sometimes even three times. I never questioned my therapist. I never asked, "How long do I have to do this to feel better?"

This is stupid. A complete waste of my time.

And then it happened. I burst open into tears. The words on the paper now appearing blurred through my clouded eyes. My writing changed, too. It no longer looked like a kid's scribble. The letters were perfectly and powerfully formed. The words and sentences neat and evenly spaced. Every sentence started and ended at the same spot on the lined notebook paper. I felt different too. Something deep inside of me shifted. Something powerful. I *can* forgive myself and reclaim that part of me that thought a guilt lunch was a good idea in the first place. In fact, I owe it to myself to do just that!

Holy shift!

Chapter 7
Legacy Loneliness

I have felt extreme loneliness in a room full of people.

Faux friendliness, synthetic smile, free-roaming thoughts, fantasies of more favorable feelings…
Why did I even come here? When can I leave? How long can I fake this? How long can they?

***

I was negatively nourished with neglect. Loneliness. It was fed through my umbilical cord. I believe it came from both sides and spanned generations. The seed was planted at conception just like the guilt spoken of earlier. My parents' resting heart rate was loneliness. Each for different reasons.

Dad was the youngest boy of eight children, two of whom were girls. He didn't join the military, go to college, hold public office, or own a liquor store like his older brothers. His job kept him close to home and mostly isolated from others. He was a letter carrier and delivered mail in all kinds of weather.

Growing up in a crowded household, I suspect the career choice was Dad's best option for escaping what must have been chaos. It was a way for him to hear his *own* thoughts and an occasional barking dog. I say *must have been chaos* because I *know* dad was an alcoholic, and I *know* three of my uncles drank as well. I suspect the others did, too, but don't know for sure because I never met them.

***

Mom had a brother, but he died as a teen, supposedly of polio. It was reported in the newspapers that way, but someone familiar with my family back then said otherwise. The family friend insisted it wasn't polio but drowning. If this were simply a one-off, I'd have likely discounted the statement as gossip. Running into that person was random enough. Then, having the conversation about how my uncle—a man I never met, died, before I was even a thought, says otherwise. When I further consider that both my mother *and* grandmother were deathly afraid of the water, *and* newspapers reported that my uncle spent five days at camp before he died, also makes drowning plausible.

Drowning can feel like a parental failure whereas a polio death can be perceived as marginally more palatable. As if that weren't enough, my grandmother started taking in foster children shortly after. I say "children" loosely to indicate she took in boys *and* girls. The truth is, she took in all boys except *one*.

***

I can't imagine losing a child. I also can't imagine if that loss *was* a potentially preventable drowning had my grandmother said "NO" to the camping trip. That's some serious guilt to grind.

I also *know* that children can't be replaced like the family dog. I can only imagine the message my grandmother's "kid shopping" sent to my mother. Insignificant? Less than? Unworthy? Useless? Let's mix in the loneliness she must have felt losing her brother, then her mother to all these other children, with the idea that boys are better. It's no surprise she eventually turned to alcohol to combat *her* childhood abandonment, neglect, and grief, just like my dad. It's also no wonder Mom and Dad found each other to perpetuate the problem.

Under the right circumstances, they both had award-winning synthetic smiles that masked the legacy loneliness their eyes *couldn't* hide. In time, their hearts couldn't beat against the aloneness anymore and gave out suddenly, Mom at forty-nine and Dad at sixty-eight.

By working hard to understand where I came from and what I was dealt, I hope to lasso the loop of love—for myself and for those courageous enough to walk the path of truth.

***

Special Note:

As I wrote the section of the chapter that spoke of my grandmother, a friend called to say she's making chuck roast for dinner. Fun fact – Chuck roast is the *only* dish my grandmother made that I didn't have to choke down like medicine. Some would say, "That's coincidence!" I say, "That's confirmation!"

Additional Update:

The following morning, I found forty-nine cents on my morning walk. That's the age Mom's heart gave out. I wonder if "some" would still say coincidence.

Chapter 8
Perpetual Pain

I've learned that languishing in loneliness has led to perpetual pain—a pain that I had to keep hidden to survive. Having been born into extreme loneliness coupled with guilt, shame, abandonment, and alcoholism, pain has been my invisible nemesis.

The life of emotional pain I've suffered up until now has had several spikes that resulted in physical conditions that tell my story. As a child, I remember having many sore throats, stomach aches, diarrhea, constipation, fevers, and bouts of vomiting. I now *know and understand* that each of these maladies surfaced from an emotional upset—an emotional upset that my parents were ill-equipped to deal with *and* my abusive, older sibling made fun of.

Dad's answer to my stomach aches was what he called "an old Indian trick." He told me to "spit on your finger and rub it on your belly button." As an innocent and trusting youngster, I believed dear old alcoholic dad and tried it several times. It never worked. Another time, I remember I was lying on the couch watching one of my favorite movies with a puke bucket next to me *and* my sibling snickering whenever our parents weren't looking. For some unknown reason, *I* was labeled the liar even though *I* was the honest, trustworthy one.

There was another time when Mom thought I was lying about not feeling well and sent me to school anyway. I remember how my classmates and I were lined up along the wall that faced the windows where the parking lot was located. We were having a spelling bee that day. It was my turn. When I opened my mouth to spell the word I was given, I vomited. It was hard to say if Mom was angry because the school called to pick me up or because she was forced to spend her day with a sick kid.

***

My *adult* medical chart continued the chronicles with additional signs through symptoms. I suffered through sprains, strains, an ulcer, a hemorrhoid, chronic knee pain, breast cancer, a ring finger dislocation, warts, a fractured foot, a thyroid condition "that cannot be corrected without medicine," high cholesterol that "I suggest you consider medication for," tooth issues*, a mysterious lump*, and chronic hip & lower back pain*.

Once I learned the spiritual body language of how emotions have affected me physically my entire life, I became more aware of how to heal myself. For instance, the sore throats and stomach aches I had as a child eventually morphed into the thyroid condition, an ulcer, and sporadic digestive issues. These were all clues I learned to interpret and heal from, one by one.

***

From the spiritual perspective, anything to do with the throat represents speaking my truth. As a child, I was taught and believed that I didn't have a voice or a choice. That belief carried into my adulthood and increased in intensity by becoming "louder" and developed into a thyroid concern "requiring medicine." My primary physician *insisted* that without taking the synthetic hormone, it would "only get worse." She was right. It did. I continued to reject taking the medicine and began writing my first book, *All My Heroes Have Fur, Fins & Feathers, An Animal Communicator's Healing Journey of Awakening*. My thyroid numbers improved—Doc remained skeptical. Upon completion of my second book, *Unraveled, From Sibling Abuse to Sacred Self,* I repeated the bloodwork. My thyroid numbers were within normal limits.

Childhood stomach aches morphed into an ulcer as other digestive and elimination issues surfaced sporadically. Stress typically presents in this area of the body and can take many forms. Interestingly, I've learned that proper digestion and assimilation don't just pertain to the foods I consume. The processes also include ideas and beliefs: mine, my family's, my peers', society's, etc. Get the picture? Not having a safe place to talk about fears and feelings wreaked havoc on my young body and continued into adulthood. Writing and talk therapy have absolutely helped my regularity, but being validated daily by peers in ACA has had even more of an effect on my well-being in this area.

The dislocation happened in the middle of a softball game, so I reset it myself and finished the game. Rest and an inflatable boot were all that were needed for the fractured foot. I opted for surgical intervention for the knee, hemorrhoid, breast cancer, and tooth issues but remain pharmaceutical-free for the thyroid and cholesterol. Truth is, I don't understand how taking medicines that have worse side effects than the original condition is a good thing. I'm not even a fan of aspirin or ibuprofen!

***

Growing up in an alcoholic and dysfunctional home has definitely had lasting physical effects on me. And thankfully, "modern medicine" is learning to consider how feelings impact physical health. Overall, my body systems seem to be working well these days. The last piece I'm actively still working on is the chronic hip and lower back pain that decided to move into my left glute and calf about a year ago. I was *finally* properly diagnosed with TMS for the recurring pain in November 2023*.

To give you an idea of how bad it was, I pulled myself out of a softball playoff game in October 2023. I also could no longer walk for my morning coffee or even around the block. Things began to improve once I was properly diagnosed and started doing the recommended homework. To date, my road to recovery has been slow and steady with the exception of two relapses. The first scared the daylights out of me and lasted for nearly two days. I could *not* get comfortable in any position except for one…being down on all fours like a dog. When my arms got tired, I'd lay my upper body on my futon. Using the toilet was also gruesome. I'd crawl into the bathroom. Rest. Then scream in agony as I hoisted myself onto the throne to do my business. Once complete, I had to rest on the floor again before crawling back into the room where I was going to hang out. It was awful. Part of the process was to keep track of successes and to get back to normal activities as fast as possible. With the second one, I knew it was coming and mentally stopped it right in its tracks! It didn't last long at all.

I've continued to experience sporadic *pains in the ass* when triggered or working through something heavy, but those events are decreasing dramatically in frequency, duration, and intensity. I have returned to all of my activities and am confident I will soon be completely pain free.

***

I am beyond grateful to the pioneers who have so boldly written and shared how emotions and trauma influence our bodies. Brene Brown's work focuses on courage, vulnerability, and shame. John E. Sarno, MD extensively documented how repressed and unconscious emotions can cause chronic pain syndromes. Bessell van der Kolk, MD researches the effects of trauma on the body and how to heal it. Dr. Gabor Mate speaks compassionately regarding how trauma, addiction, stress, abandonment, and childhood development affect our thought processes and behaviors. Louise Haye beautifully spells out where emotions can lead our bodies into states of dis-ease and powerful affirmations that can bring ourselves back into balance. The trailblazing works by these individuals has helped me navigate my perpetual pain in a way that makes me realize that I am neither crazy nor broken. Their tools have empowered me in a way few others have.

*These physical concerns were introduced in my second book, Unraveled: From Sibling Abuse to Sacred Self. I concluded it was likely Tension Myositis Syndrome (TMS), but that book went to print before the official diagnosis and treatment plan.

Chapter 9
Silent Screams

Deafening.
My silent screams were deafening.
In my own head.
Why doesn't anyone else hear them?

***

Tearfully, I can remember recurrent childhood nightmares of being chased, bound, drowned, locked in dark places, and so much more. As I recall those terror loops today, I realize that my nightmares as a kid were me reliving my real-life daytime drama. As an adult replaying the memories of that time period, I notice the immediate changes in my physical body. Adrenaline surges through my system like water from a fire hose as my body moves into survival mode. My heart races, muscles tense, and my breathing becomes shallow... still... almost sixty years later. THIS is the type of childhood trauma that causes CPTSD (Complex Post Traumatic Stress Disorder). THESE experiences were repeatedly instigated by my one and only sibling. They reek of pure evil.

Vividly, I recall the terror and helplessness my younger self felt at the hands of a two-headed monster—two-headed because what others see still remains very different from the person I saw.

During the incidents, attempts at screaming for help were silenced with either fearful threats or the covering of my mouth with a hand, tied gag, or pillow. Nighttime "dream" screams were different. I can remember telling myself to take a deep breath so I could scream loud and long. When I opened my mouth and engaged my screaming muscles, nothing happened. No sound would come out. I'd wake with a sore throat as though I had screamed all night.

Inside my head, the screams were deafening, so shrill they would cause the thickest glass to shatter. They were a primal call for attention…for *help*. As I reflect on the experiences, I wonder whether either of my parents would have done anything had they heard me. At some point, I stopped screaming and stopped fighting. My life purpose became taking whatever was dished from whoever was dishing, especially in my close relationships. Internally, I became a hollow shell. Externally, I faked so much of my existence so that I would be likeable, safe, under the radar. Eventually, I found alcohol and became a blackout drinker to sleep and cope.

All that childhood trauma was inside festering like poison in my mind, body and soul. But I didn't dare talk about it, so I drank to try and drown it out. I barely remember staggering home one night and passing out hard, half-undressed, half in the bed and half out. I must have had just enough alcohol in me to relax into my night terror. I can't recall which one it was, but I do remember the seal on my scream being broken. The deafening scream I heard leave my own body was no longer silent. It woke and sobered me up like a slap across the face. Whatever was holding back my screams had finally let loose.

Chapter 10
Fighting Back the Fears

I remember the apartment.

A small two-bedroom on the second floor owned by a nasty drunk. I remember overhearing the adults say that he regularly beat up his wife. A dark wooden staircase leading up to the apartment had a landing and ninety-degree turn halfway up. It opened to a hallway off which all the rooms connected. To the right of the stairs were the two bedrooms, and to the left, the bathroom, kitchen, tiny living room and a door that led to the creepiest of walk-up attics. The bedroom that eventually became mine was on one end of the hallway, and the kitchen was on the other.

I remember how old I was.

Seven years separated my older sibling and me. Since I was "the baby," and the apartment only had two bedrooms, I was stuck sleeping with my snoring, overweight, alcohol drinking, cigarette smoking mother...until the day I no longer had to. Visitation Thursday. Dad came to get us. My recently-turned-sixteen sibling had all their things packed to move in with Dad. Elated doesn't even begin to describe the excitement of not having to share a bed with my mother anymore. I can still remember the sheer joy of jumping up and down on the bed like a circus performer as I shouted to the world, "I HAVE MY OWN ROOM!" To say it was the best surprise of my childhood would not be an understatement. It was 1973. I was nine.

I remember the scene.

Loud voices, not snoring, woke me from a sound sleep. I stumbled out of bed wearing a too-big-for-me pair of hand-me-downs, nearly worn-through, vertically striped, flannel, boy's pajamas. Shuffling down the smokey hallway I heard boisterous laughter. It felt like the middle of the night. Clearly, it was late because the babysitter was gone. The closer I got to the kitchen, the thicker the cigarette smoke and the more raucous the racket. It was drunk laughter. I froze in the doorway. Seated at the kitchen table were my mother, her then boyfriend, another woman, and one of Manville's finest—a high ranking police official. On the table were smoking, cigarette-filled ashtrays, bottles of beer, and a loaded gun. It was laying on its side with the business end pointed in the direction of where I was standing. The laughter stopped. "GET BACK IN BED!" My mother spat.

I remember the fear.

Guns are dangerous. Guns kill people. There's a gun in my house! I'm scared. What's going to happen to me? I was terrified. My body was trembling with fear. *The police are supposed to protect me—what's going on here?* I clung to my bed blankets and listened intently for any sign of danger. Eventually, exhaustion took over and I fitfully fell back to sleep.

I remember the trigger.

I was in my early 40's. The woman I was dating was in federal law enforcement. She was suffering unusual fatigue that took some time to properly diagnose and treat. As the condition progressed, she would sometimes become confused and disoriented. It was during one of those episodes that my gun fear was triggered. When I arrived at her house, she was standing at the foot of her bed looking helplessly at her service weapon in pieces before her on the mattress. "I don't know what to do," she said. "I can't remember how it goes back together." Just like the nine-year-old Sherri, I froze. Those gun "pieces" had just as much of a legacy loop on me as the loaded one did all those years before. The jolt felt like I was a dog jerked while wearing a prong collar. I still can't recall how the rest of that day played out, but I do know how helpless I felt. Again.

***

Over time, I dated other women who carried and eventually went to an indoor shooting range for a crash course with a male cop friend. I appreciated his offer and willingness, but I left there still feeling fearful and ill-prepared. *Oh well, I can't be an expert at everything.*

***

I remember saying YES!

A dear friend asked if I would attend a women's only gun class with her. I tearfully told the story of my childhood gun trauma and forced a deep cleansing breath. *You're safe Sherri, you're safe. You can do this.* I steadied myself and responded YES! It's time to fight back the fears.

Chapter 11
Adulting and Accountability

I did a thing today.
A *very* courageous thing.
An adult thing.
A *very* adult thing.
I held myself accountable.

***

She'd been on my mind. A lot. I wondered how things were going with her. She sent the last text over a year and a half ago. I didn't respond. I couldn't. I was adjusting to life without her and learning how my childhood trauma caused me to unconsciously choose relationships that mirrored that unhealthy environment. I was on unsteady ground and needed time to regain my footing. And that's what I did. Self-care.

***

For months, I had attended more ACA meetings than there are days in the week. I focused on my healing and was finally emotionally ready to reach out. I was ready to hold myself accountable for not acknowledging the harmless holiday greeting that seared my heart like a branding iron. It was time for me to extract the embedded fist I also physically felt from the perceived sucker punch.

I thought about it, talked about it, and slept on it…for weeks. I asked for divine guidance and pulled oracle cards. Carefully and truthfully, I considered my motives and possible outcome(s).

What do I hope to gain? What are the pros and cons? Will I be able to handle her response or non-response?

Whenever *my* thoughts strayed to how *she* might feel, I reeled myself back in. *I am responsible for managing my own feelings, not anyone else's, not ever.* I've learned there is an emotional boundary present in healthy relationships of all kinds.

True and lasting intimacy is creating a safe space for all thoughts and feelings to be expressed and discussed fearlessly, not just the good ones. Faux feelings and communication rooted in fear of upsetting another are most present in co-dependent, symbiotic, and superficial relationships. I've had those kinds of relationships. They were my familiars and no longer work for me. *My* journey is one of growth and taking healthy risks…so I took one.

Much thought went into my long-delayed response.

I may only get one chance at this; what do I need to say? What is my truth? I want it to be short and sweet and completely honest. What if she…STOP IT, that's not yours to manage…stay in your lane!

How do I do this? Text? Email? Hand-written letter?

A card! That's it! An "I'm sorry" card!

I went to three different stores. There were zero "I'm sorry" cards. *People just don't apologize anymore, I guess.* I found the perfect "Thinking of You" card. My words were ready days before I found an appropriate card. This was a big deal for me. An extremely courageous act. No one in my family of origin ever modeled accountability, much less apologized, explained or attempted to open a closed door. No one ever.

Apologizing sincerely is an intimate acknowledgement of someone else's heart. It is a way of communicating, "you and our relationship matter to me." My intention was to do just that. *I* needed to apologize for not responding and be accountable for my actions or in this case, inaction. I also wanted to let her know my door was open for further discussion. Essentially, I took a very bold step and extended an olive branch.

I nervously and lovingly wrote out the card, addressed the envelope, and walked it to the post office. Before depositing my heartfelt message in the mail slot, I called in my spirit guides and blessed the process. As best as I could in that moment, I detached, with love, from any particular outcome. The moment was incredibly emotional and moving for me. Outwardly exposing my vulnerable side was a healthy risk I was consciously ready to take. I felt safe enough to take the chance. And did. There was no second guessing my choice. Not one shred of regret or wishing I'd written more, or less. My message was perfect and my intention pure.

***

Cue *The Twilight Zone* music. Her lengthy response, via text, came while I was attending an author event. The last time I did the event she was there, lovingly supporting me and the other writers. The synchronistic timing had me eager to read her reply immediately.

Chapter 12
The Response

The timing. OMG! The timing. It's a sign. A GOOD sign!
Everything around me stopped and went dark, like someone pressed the "pause" button, and I entered a black hole. It felt as if the only thing that existed in that dreamy space was me, the chair I was sitting on, and the phone I lovingly held in my hands. It was as if *she* were actually *in* the phone. I was no longer at an author event surrounded by dozens of people. The chatter of others had vanished. It felt warm, loving, and safe. I *had* to read her response. *Right now*!

My body was pulsing with the excited anticipation of a favorable response. *She wondered about me as well! Why else would she respond? And so quickly too!*

***

Her response was carefully crafted using the sandwich method. This method involves two upbeat comments serving as the bread with the not so tasty meat *sandwiched* in the middle. She started with something positive to get my attention, filled the middle with stuff that was uncomfortable and unresolved between us, and finished with good wishes for my fur babies so that I wouldn't be left with a nasty taste in my mouth. Some of what she wrote I could and would have easily conceded to—given the chance to have a conversation. I *know* I don't have the memory I had when I was younger. I also know that some of the other things she wrote I could have validated for her even *if* I didn't feel the same way. I've learned in the last year and a half that that is how people who care and respect one another agree to disagree. It is healthy.

The first time I read the message, I went numb. I somberly turned to my friend at the author event and said, "I just heard from her." My body began to tremble as I fought back tears.

This can't be happening. It's like being broken up with all over again.

"Do you need to take a minute for yourself? Go ahead, I've got this," my friend said.

I got up and ran to the ladies' room. Just like almost every other ladies' room I've ever been to, there was a line. Hiding in a stall and doing an ugly girl cry was not an option. There was really no other place for me to hide for the last twenty minutes of the event, so I just sat there expressionless, feeling hollow and gutted. It felt incredibly isolating and familiar. I felt abandoned. Again.

My friend and I packed up our stuff and walked to her car several blocks away. Eventually, I mustered the courage to read the response again, out loud, in the company of someone who's known me a very long time. I felt safe to shed my tears and thoughts as we drove to where my car was parked. We agreed that the overall message was written kindly, without malice, and that she was not interested in discussion of any kind. Our takeaway was that she had closed the door, and I didn't have to respond to her response. It was done, and I was sad. "I feel like I've lost her all over again," I sniffled to my friend. "This just sucks."

***

Over the coming days, I read the message several more times at different times of the day and night. One phrase reverberated in my head. Even though it was a text, I could imagine being in her presence as she said it…without making eye contact…coupled with her "tell" which is a nervous leg shake. "Our boundaries just don't line up."

Should they? Isn't that the point of boundaries?

I observed how my emotions were all over the place. I cycled from hopeful, to surprised, to hurting, to hurting *for her,* to reflective, to unguarded, to disappointed, to sad. The emotional cycling was painstakingly leading me through another round of grief toward acceptance.

I considered responding but didn't want to wind up in a word war, furiously going back and forth tit for tat. That's something I would have done prior to ACA recovery. *That* communication style came from my family of origin. It's not healthy to cowardly shoot messages back and forth with someone, eagerly sitting on the edge of my seat waiting for some kind of response. I've learned that's not adulting; it's crazy making. As hard as it was, I began to move into acceptance. I also took time to celebrate the healthy risk I *consciously chose* to make… to be accountable for my behavior. And did.

A few days later, I noticed she sent me a friend request in Facebook. "Old me" would have wholeheartedly and haphazardly accepted it immediately; like a pigeon pining for a stray crumb. "New me" was like "WTF? I'm working on acceptance and now the game seems to have changed again…*without* a heads up or conversation?" *Talk about mixed messages. This feels eerily familiar. This is how my psycho sibling operated… and my crazy workplace… do this… no, don't do this… jump… no, don't jump… jump higher. The ground beneath my feet was moving again. How does this make me feel? What do I do? Sit Sherri… you don't have to make a decision right this minute. Just sit.*

And sit I did. I sat and asked for divine guidance. I spoke with trusted friends. I wrote about it. I thought about it. I thought about sending a message asking for clarification and was working through the wording in my head. I wanted a degree of clarity before deciding whether to accept the friend request or not. And then it was gone. I don't know exactly how long the request was there, but I'm fairly certain on the third day it was gone.

Our boundaries just don't line up.

Should they?

Chapter 13
Boundaries and Beliefs

I'm a ChapStick-wearing, sports-playing lesbian. Up until a few years ago, the only thing I knew about boundaries had to do with foul lines, the 3' x 7' softball batter's box, and more recently the kitchen as it relates to a Pickleball court. Being visual, every time I *heard* the word boundary, the athlete inside of me saw perfectly-maintained, *boundary*-lined sports fields. Doesn't everybody? I believed that everybody saw things the exact same way I did and *not* through their *own* lens.

Lipstick-wearing, snack-toting, sports-supporting is the opposite type of lesbian. Opposites attract. Right?

She's an educator. She's smarter and more organized than you. She knows better.

***

Our boundaries don't line up.
Should they?

***

As a child, choices were taken away from me and poor behavior was modeled. It's what I saw. And learned. I am a visual, hands-on learner. My belief was that that's how everybody learned. I've since discovered that I was living in survival mode. Asking questions as a child got me ridiculed, yelled at, or beaten. It was just not safe to ask questions, much less ask for something or say no. Lessons *I* received came from the school of hard knocks through trial and error, watching others, and shamefully, believing just about every single thing I heard.

After graduating high school, picking up a book was a concept about as far away from me as Mars. *Why would anyone want to read after being forced to all through school?* That's certainly funny to me now but wasn't so much then. Now, I read for pleasure, to learn, and more importantly, to grow. I've read more books these last few years than *all* my years in school…and I'm still reading, learning, and growing.

***

Our boundaries don't line up.
Should they?

***

The question sputtered on spin in my cerebrum.
Should they?

***

The instant *New York Times* best seller, *Set Boundaries, Find Peace - A Guide to Reclaiming Yourself* written by licensed therapist and relationship expert Nedra Glover Tawwab found its way into my hands. One of the back cover reviews referred to it as the "boundary bible." From cover to cover, this book provided the insight and information that exceeded my expectations. I received far more than the simple answer I was looking for.

I saw myself in the pages. I also saw people I know, love, and respect in the pages. All of us were on both sides of the boundary dilemma that wreaks havoc in relationships of all kinds. I was similarly shocked to see that I have been a boundary violator *AND* someone who needs to do a much better job of setting and enforcing my own. It's no coincidence either that some of the stories use names familiar to me, just to drive the points home! To make matters better (or worse), boundaries aren't always transparent like ChapStick and sports fields. Oh no, according to the Self-Assessment Quiz in the back of the book, boundaries can be porous, rigid or healthy.

It is impossible to dress up poor or non-existent boundaries with lipstick and call them a boundary. That's called fear.

Our boundaries just don't line up.
Should they?
Absolutely NOT! Not even if we were conjoined twins.

***

*Special note – The draft of this chapter resulted in 555 words. 555 is an incredibly powerful number representing change, good luck, transformation, freedom, and personal growth. It is validation for the courageous work I am undertaking.

Chapter 14

It's Just a Carpet Anyway

June 26, 2024

I replaced the carpeting in the room I affectionately called the big living room. The stain fighter protection had been shampooed out long ago, rendering the room's rug way beyond cleaning. It felt tattered, tired, and filthy. My once-luxurious floor covering had become legacy loops dotted with pet puke stains and torn by cat claws. The final flaw left an ever-growing gap in the middle of the room—much like the divide between family members. Like the exhausted enabler in a dysfunctional household, the carpet's seam tape could no longer hold the pieces together. Its time had come.

It's just a carpet anyway.

***

August 28, 1990

It was the cheapest house around—situated next to a nuisance business in a not-so-great neighborhood. I was eleven days shy of my twenty-sixth birthday and had been "living" in my father's unfinished basement while my older sibling and two children happily scampered above my head on the main level. The handyman's special I was about to move into with dirty, sculpted, navy blue, grease-stained carpet in the big living room was a definite step up. It didn't matter that I could see my *new* basement below while sitting on the main bathroom's toilet or the obvious omission of a silverware drawer in the dated, dysfunctional kitchen.

I didn't have either of those things in Dad's dank dungeon either.

Hearing vehicular and foot traffic not far from my front window was a welcome change from the sometimes-purposeful heel pounding of the "people" walking above my head on the hardwood floors. Having grown up with this spiteful sibling, I *knew* their kids often took their cues from their parasitic parent who spent the majority of their life living free under Dad's roof. Snoozing on the cleanest section of that caustic and contaminated carpet in my sleeping bag felt dreamy and safe. It took weeks before the place felt clean enough to bring my twin mattress and eventually some basic furniture for the smaller room that initially served as a living room. *I* was now a homeowner without any help from anybody.

***

Just about every nickel I had went into the down payment. There were very few reserves. Items were prioritized and completed slowly as I was able to afford them. For instance, I considered viewing the basement while seated on the toilet a feature, whereas living without a silverware drawer was not. My motto back then was, "If it's free, it's for me." To that end, my kitchen cabinets were fashioned from old pallets that were used to ship windows for a huge construction project near my job. The guy I was dating at the time and I went dumpster diving to repurpose them. I had the painstaking job of removing all the Styrofoam and staples while he disassembled and rejoined, planed, and sanded the pallet slats to create beautiful cabinets, complete with a silverware drawer, for my now functional kitchen.

Two five-gallon spackle buckets and a piece of plywood served as our table. And that nasty blue carpet served as our seating. The Swanson Hungry Man Turkey TV dinners never tasted so good. We were so happy and content. The house was cleaning up nicely, and it was time to tear up those threads and see what was below.

It's just a carpet anyway.

***

July 4, 2024 – Independence Day
Finding freedom from dysfunction has required me to take an honest look back at why seemingly-benign events cause internal fireworks for me today. It is a necessary part of my healing process. For some, replacing carpet is a simple, ordinary task. For me, a trauma survivor with complex PTSD who is

working hard to repair my faulty circuitry, it became a monumental mission with several spokes. I had to mentally and emotionally ride out each of the figurative spokes to bring my legacy-looped carpet stories full circle.

July 4, 2024 – UPDATE: To celebrate the completion of this chapter, I went for a head-clearing walk. I acknowledged how present-day me feels about having "lived" in an unfinished basement. The emotions and thoughts were mixed. I cried for that part of me that acknowledged I've had strangers treat me better than the important people in my life back then. I also celebrated the survivor in me that used that basement as a stepping-stone to create a safer place to live. Lastly, I thought about those heel-stomping children who are now in their forties. Have either of them come around to the idea that it isn't remotely normal for a family member to live in an unfinished basement? I received my answer in coins. Eight dimes to be exact. Four and four. One of those heel-stompers was born exactly forty-four years ago today. My higher self immediately reached out to theirs…

Now that you know the truth, what are you going to do about it?

*According to a *Psychology Today* article posted on March 23, 2023 regarding "Adverse Childhood Experiences and 8 Common Dysfunctional Family Roles", The enabler or caretaker: the person who maintains the look or appearance of normalcy within the family. They support and affirm the unhealthy behavior of other family members…

Chapter 15

The Spokes Speak

Many of the "spokes" aren't straight and are of varied length. Some dangle desperately in the wind, reaching helplessly for the stability of the rim, similarly to how a confused child with outstretched arms reaches toward a loving caregiver seeking safety and comfort. The wheel of the tired tale that the spokes speak has also long lost its shape. It is mangled and rusted and mirrors a bike wheel run over by the family car several times before being discarded in the river. It makes no matter. Those bike spokes still speak to the weary wanderer wheeling toward healing.

***

The first house I lived in as a child had no carpet. *That* was a luxury we couldn't afford. It *had* beautiful hard wood floors that made running in socks and sliding down the hallway fun. Colorful, string-fringed rag rugs marked the front and back doors. Over time, through use and abuse, harsh cleaning and non-existent maintenance, those once shiny and smooth planks began looking lusterless and unloved, much like me.

My second matted memory was the area rug that hid beneath the table in my maternal grandmother's dimly-lit dining room. Its edges were framed with grubby gold tassels, many of which were tangled like discarded hair caught in a shower drain. Looking back, I believe the poor lighting of that room was purposeful. It concealed the room's dusty furniture and massive amounts of pet fur woven into the carpet's threads. Many years later, as an ambitious teenager who wanted to try out a carpet shampooer, I was absolutely appalled by what was revealed when the dimmer dial on the crystal chandelier was spun! *Shit! We actually ate in here! How disgusting! This makes the* Munster's *living room look spotless!*

Another disturbing incident involving carpet threads occurred while living in the same place I was molested for the first time. To add to my already complex childhood traumas, this incident also involved animal abuse. My mother, her on-again, off-again boyfriend Jack, and I lived in an apartment just over the railroad tracks from my hometown for about a year. Just like some couples struggling in a relationship think having kids will bring them closer together, these two lovebirds decided purchasing a silver poodle puppy from a local breeder was a good idea. They named him Muffin.

The three of us had gone out for the day and left the new puppy home alone, uncrated, to do as he wished. Upon returning home, we found that Muffin had dug out a loose thread from the wall-to-wall carpeting in the corner nearest the entry door and adjacent coat closet. In our absence, the bored pup pulled rows of looped carpet from the mesh that kept it bound. Furious, Jack forcefully pushed the pup's face into the threadbare section and screamed, "WHAT IS THIS? BAD DOG!!!" Terrified and shaking with his puny puppy tail tucked far up between his back legs, Muffin fearfully peed in place. Jack wasn't finished. He angrily grabbed Muffin by the scruff of the neck and drop-kicked him into the closet like a football. From that moment on, the pup and I were never the same. He inappropriately peed everywhere, and *we* lived a life in fear. Eleven-year-old me remained silent and did as I was told lest I'd be drop-kicked in the closet too! I already related too closely with being cornered, beaten, and screamed at inappropriately. The sound Muffin's body made when it connected with the back of the closet and the simultaneous "YIPE" were looped into my carpet memory cellular circuitry so deeply that the molestation that occurred here paled by comparison. This "spoke" may have been short, but the rusty and jagged edges will require tender loving self-care, just like the barnacles on the bottom of a long-forgotten boat.

***

One of the other places the three of us lived had inexpensive, speckled, thinly padded carpeting in every room except the bathroom. That crappy carpeting was even in the kitchen! I can't place if we lived there before or after the place mentioned in the paragraph above. Trauma does that.

Multiple traumas don't fall predictably, one at a time, like a neatly placed soldiering of dominos. Incidents for multiple trauma survivors can trigger, such as the grand finale of a pyrotechnics show with misfiring memories shooting like hot rockets in every direction. Sometimes my buried memories ricochet off each other like multiple balls in a pinball machine, ringing invisible bells that send my internals into sensory overload. They certainly aren't always linear, and sometimes something completely unrelated will light the fuse for a series of flashbacks. To that end, the story above set off one of those flashbacks.

***

I had been *over*-punished; banished to my non-airconditioned, hotter than hell bedroom upstairs…immediately. There was no conversation or explanation—I was just supposed to *know by now*. It was damn near impossible to decipher what I did or didn't do and why I was even in trouble—and didn't dare ask. It never took much to unhinge my mother. The mention of "inappropriate pee and living a life in fear" in the previous paragraph spawned this hellacious spoke. Soon after being sent upstairs, I realized my bladder was full. It wasn't the "I'm going to use this as an excuse to tiptoe downstairs and try and make nice" kind of motivation. I really had to go pee! I remember standing at the top of the stairs and pausing. I wondered how *this* was going to go over. "Ma?" I hesitated…"MA!", I said a little louder. "MA! I have to go to the bathroom…BAD…can I come down? Please? I'm sorry…I won't do it again" I said the words even though I didn't have the foggiest idea of what I even had done. "Ma?"

I could hear her fat feet…heels pounding angrily on the cheap carpeting below as she approached the base of the stairs. "YOU'RE **NOT** COMING DOWN HERE…PEE IN THE POT!" My mother, a short, flabby couch potato, held the handle of a small sauce pot in her right hand while I looked pleadingly down the dimly-lit stairs at her. I didn't need better lighting to know the expression she was sporting. And her angry energy reached me long before her words. She whipped a pot up the stairs at my shins. It was the pot I used to heat up my soup. Having no other options, I peed in that pot. I poured my pee out the second-floor window onto the first-floor overhang that faced the street. And cried myself to sleep.

***

The last place the three of us lived together was the home for which my grandmother gave my mother the downpayment. A crappy little house with small rooms and only one tiny closet, it was likely the cheapest available since Gram was a miser. Twisting twin spokes to tell this home's tale would keep much of my trauma tamed. In fact, braided telecom wires from a third world country couldn't serve as an adequate visual. *This* "home" was also where I eventually found my mother dead, the molestation continued, and so much more. Those spokes are in other chapters or other books. I'll try and stick to the floor covering. Similar to the house in the previous paragraph, this one also had cheap, poorly-padded, speckled carpeting. The speckling concealed dirt and offered camouflage to fleas. Since Muffin was never professionally groomed, his fur attracted fleas like a giant magnet. Because I had a board across the entrance to my miniscule room off the kitchen to keep his flea infested fur and leg-lifting self out of my bedroom, his fleas took up residence in the living room carpet. I discovered this one day while walking through in my then-popular white, with three colored stripes at the top, tube socks. I felt prickly pinches on my calves. Like the flooring dotted with cat puke that commenced the carpet stories in the first place, my white socks were noticeably dotted with black fleas. They tunneled their way through to their meal of my legs. Just like the faux face of my family of origin, what appeared clean at the surface, was anything but.

Shame and fear kept these stories buried. Courage finally arrived, and the spokes began to speak.

Chapter16
Treading the Threads

As a child, treading the threads lightly was how I survived. After my angry, pee-pot-throwing mother died, I began to learn and practice something she never learned. Patience.

***

The first carpet I ever bought for myself was a remnant. Its unbound, frayed edges represented much of my life experience up to that point; exposed and unsecured. I was drawn to choose a warm, internally soothing color that was in the red family. The exact name is insignificant, but I recall it was somewhere in the palate between mauve and cranberry. In Reiki, red is the color of the first chakra and represents one's feelings of safety and security. This remnant would warm the cold cement floor and mark the hub of my new "safe" area in Dad's unfinished basement. I waterproofed two cinder block walls white, slid a large bookcase into place to mark a third "wall", and purchased an inexpensive fiberboard armoire to serve both as a closet and partial fourth wall. A local electrician installed outlets, and I secured my very own phone service. To complete the living space, I plugged in a light. It was a clamp lamp as bright as one used in an interrogation room. For ease of use, I attached it to my bed's headboard. Lastly, I made a deal with the spirits I was terrified of as a youngster. *I won't be here any longer than I have to…you stay on your side, and I'll stay on mine.* These were the same spirits I met as a youngster when locked in the dark basement by my older sibling.

My second purchased floor covering was much nicer. It was a seven-by-nine-foot area rug complete with bound edges and framed with a sculpted design around the perimeter. The majority of it was cranberry, which was set off by two slim bands of ivory and green near the outside borders. Ironically, this "nicer" carpet was the first one I bought for my new home. It replaced the remnant that made the move to this house. That area rug was also replaced a few years ago with one that truly represents the animal and nature lover in me. The largest portion is in the ivory family, but *this* area rug is framed in brown and gray earth tones. What makes it more "me" is that two corners have a bear in the design, and the other two have a moose. Sitting in the room where this carpet rests makes me feel like I'm in a cabin in the woods…and *that* soothes my soul.

November 11, 1992

I am an earth girl. Looking back, I always have been. I love being outside…in any kind of weather. When I can't be outside, I want to be on the floor, but not on a bare floor—I guess I'm used to "cover ups." Much had happened in the two years since I bought the handyman's special. The guy I went dumpster diving with beat the crap out of me after a good night of drinking. It happened shortly after we removed the dirty blue carpet used as seating for our romantic TV-dinner dining experience. To protect myself, I kicked him out. In time, a woman would become my next partner. The room was freshly painted, and the floor was clean, but not so appealing. It had the same kind of tile as my high school hallways. I purchased my very first wall-to-wall carpet, solid light grey with the very best padding available. Cash discount. I absolutely *loved* that carpet and how warm and safe it made that whole room feel.

1993 through Easter, 2017

That beautiful, well-maintained carpet absorbed an enormous amount of love, life, and laughter. From friends and family to cats and kids, we did all kinds of things on that carpet. Catch and fetch with the cats, nerf baseball and volleyball, game and movie nights with friends and family, chicken fights on our knees, blanket forts, camping and sleepovers with the twins, and eventually their younger sibling, and so much more. It was also the most restorative room in my home. Nearly every person who was struggling with something would easily fall asleep, mid-sentence, in that room. That's a really big deal for anyone who struggles with feeling safe.

Fall, 2017

Laughter started to leave, and the stain fighter began losing its fight. The cat puke became more prominent. Like the enabler in a dysfunctional family, the carpet-seam tape was also beginning to give up. I too, was giving up...on my worthiness of love *and* my family of origin. I began to give up on anyone actually keeping their promises and treating me decently. No one liked my recent uncovering of truth. I also found it uglier than the dirty blue carpet *and* the tile beneath it. The truth that had people scattering like bugs when a light is turned on was the announcement that my one and only sibling repeatedly abused me throughout childhood. That once luxurious and comforting carpet would start to play a different role. It would have to absorb each tear and fear as I struggled to find a forward gear.

Winter 2017 through 2022

As I slowly worked through my healing process, the carpet became more tattered and tired. The divide between the two sides of the seam tape grew further and further apart—just like my family. I didn't have the mental or emotional bandwidth to make big decisions for quite a while. I was grieving the loss of my entire living family and eventually, the childhood I didn't have. Like me, the carpet could no longer hold on to what was. It had to go. But it couldn't go right away. There were dirty projects in, around, and above that room that had to be completed first. While my emotional house was being cleaned and rebuilt, so was my physical house. I invested in a new roof, the removal, clean up and replacement of attic insulation, and a new front window.

2024

The last messy item to be completed was a refresh of the half bath off the big living room. It is the smallest room in the house; I could stretch out my arms in a "T" in either direction and touch the walls. Despite its size, this room was absolutely the biggest pain in the ass to redo...especially for a fussy Virgo like myself. To give you an idea of the silliest of obstacles with the project, it took ten people, four different types of saws, three home improvement stores, and multiple days to secure, cut, and install seven feet of trim to match the piece on the back wall that ran *through* the side wall! Seven feet of trim! The room had a beautiful, ornate, painted, copper ceiling that was a nightmare to re-fresh, uneven and banged up walls, and an outdated, sun-stained linoleum tile floor. Logic dictated this room's completion *before* the nice, new, clean, carpet install. *At least the fixtures don't need replacing.* Each time something wasn't going smoothly, I'd close the door and walk away.

Patience, Sherri, patience. It will get done when it gets done.

Chapter 17

Bathroom Shit Show

Finally! The bathroom ceiling, walls, doors, and trim were refreshed to my satisfaction. This was a looooong time coming. Shopping for the big living room carpet and bathroom floor put me into the home stretch, or so I thought. The first price I was quoted for the carpet had me wondering if it was threaded with real gold. It was over *nine times* what I paid to have the room carpeted the first time. Of course, the "helpful" saleslady brought me to the Cadillac of carpets section first! "What room are *we* looking for flooring for?" she initially asked. I heard my snarky inner teen reply inside my head…and smiled. *We aren't doing anything together.* Eventually, *we* found a suitable, less-expensive option and moved on to the laminates for the bathroom.

While we walked to the other area of the store, me, quietly, in sneakers and her, noisily with the clickity-clack of high heels, the snooty saleswoman announced that the *starting price* for installing my 4x5 bathroom would be $500. I spontaneously laughed out loud thinking she was joking. The poker face response to my laughter told me she was dead serious. I put my arms out in a "T" as I said, "Lady, my bathroom is this big…$500 for installation, you have to be kidding!" She leaned in close and batted her eyes as if she were sharing some great, big, trade secret. "Well, you know…most people have a bigger bathroom." I could *hear* my inner teenager tell my adult self to step aside. *I'll handle her.* My adult self leaned in toward her and wondered just how my playful, inner teen was going to counter. "Just so *you* know, I would gladly pay more for installation if I *had* a bigger bathroom."

Our pissing match continued. With eyebrows arched and eyes cast downward; the saleslady folded her scrawny arms across her chest while trying desperately to defend the ridiculous installation cost. I paid very close attention to the woman's body language. The inability to maintain eye contact and crossed arms spoke more truth than her words ever would. "Well, you know, the floor installer is different from the carpet installer." Of course, my inner teen countered with, "Well, just so *you* know, when I was still working, I knew how to do more than one thing…AND, my people know how to pull a toilet. I can easily install the flooring myself." And I walked out laughing. *$500 for 20 square feet of flooring! Eff that! How hard could this be? The effing room is small and square!* After shopping at two large home improvement stores that wanted nearly eighty bucks a box for just under 20 square feet, I scored a thirty-dollar box for 27 square feet at the Restore!

Patience and persistence are paying off. I know how to pull a fucking toilet!

***

I coordinated a floor installation date with a friend who loves *any* excuse to use her oscillating tool and began the last of the half-bath prep. Carefully, I removed the existing quarter round trim that rested just above the edges of the now hideous-looking peel and stick tile. My plan was to pull the toilet at the last possible moment to shorten the time it would be out of service. How long could it possibly take to install twenty square feet of flooring in a square bathroom? *We're in the home stretch!*

Never having installed this kind of flooring, I was excited to learn. Just before my friend arrived, I shut off the water supply, removed the tank cover and flushed. After the first flush, I followed with a bucket of water. The extra bucket directly poured into the bowl creates a suction that causes the rest of the contents to be sucked down the drain. I used a sponge to absorb the water in the tank and the last bit in the bowl. The water supply hose was disconnected and the johnny bolt caps wiggled off. Once exposed, the bolts holding the bowl in place were removed. It was time to pull the toilet! The whole process couldn't have taken five minutes. I gave my toilet a bear hug and began to lift. It wouldn't come up! Caulk still had a grip on it. I handily used my utility knife to separate the toilet from the linoleum tile and tried again. Success! *WOOHOO! This is exciting! Perfect timing, my friend was on her way.*

***

I had questions.

"Should we pull up the old tile? Will the johnny bolts be long enough with the new floor."

Her responses were, "No and we have bolts with the new wax seal…we should be good."

"Where do we start? At the back and move toward the door or at the door and move toward the wall?"

"At the wall…the first piece will be a partial piece since the planks have to be installed staggered…got a tape measure"?

The initial two pieces were easy peasy since the only cuts were relatively straight. Our next plank was a bit of a nail biter for me because it had two curved cuts, and it was obvious that the oscillating tool blade was pretty beat up from previous projects. "You got any other saws"?

I fetched both my jigsaw and scroll saw and we soldiered on. The water supply notch and half the hole for the toilet waste pipe were cut, and the piece slid in place. I breathed a sigh of relief knowing we have a little wiggle room with planks, but there was only one box of the color I wanted. The next cut was for the *other* half of the toilet hole. "You got more blades? This one snapped." Smiling that indeed, I *did have* more blades, I retreated to retrieve them. *Homestretch…we are in the homestretch…after this piece, they're all pretty straight.*

As we neared the doorway, the plank that would be in this position needed to be cut lengthwise as well as trimmed to match the door frame. We had only one "extra" piece to play with. It didn't go well. The wall wasn't as straight as we thought it was; the cuts were off, and we came up short.

"I guess we're going to wait for Eric to get home, huh…. since we only have one piece to play with?"

"Yep."

***

The look on his face told me we should have started at the door. Just like the saleslady, he couldn't make eye contact with either one of us. A gentle, loving man, he would never make either one of us feel bad for trying to do it on our own…he'd just make it right. We'd get our chops busted sometime later…but definitely not now. He ripped up what we did, restarted at the door, and got the floor and new quarter round trim installed beautifully! *We are in the homestretch! Just have to reseat the toilet!*

"Hey, let's dry fit the toilet before putting the seal in there to make sure the johnny bolts are still long enough" I suggested. My gut felt like they wouldn't be.

They weren't.

My friend's husband had never seen the kind of flange my toilet had and wasn't comfortable with the next step. Grateful for their help with the floor, I was on my own for the next phase of the shit show.

Fucking bathroom…

The floor looks nice!

I closed the door and walked away.

Chapter 18
Progress Not Perfection

Progress not perfection.
Easy does it.
YOU CAN DO THIS!
Ask for help.

***

Program slogans and affirmations were swirling around in my head. They were a far cry from the harsh and nasty things I *would* have been thinking and saying to myself *before* walking into the rooms of ACA. Prior to learning how my inner critical parent tainted my thoughts, I'd have been verbally assaulting and judging myself for *not* having the "fucking bathroom" done yet. All the soul stealing messages that were shouted and beaten into me as a child would have easily echoed eerily in the space between my ears. My body would have felt that same childhood tension while trying to ignore feeling helpless, useless, worthless, and stupid. Stupid for even *trying* to take on a project like this in the first place.

Who do you think you are? What were you thinking? You can't do that.

The *new* voice inside my head is that of a gentle, patient, loving and encouraging parent, the one I deserved but never had.

I can learn to be gentle with myself! I AM being gentle with myself! WHOA!

***

Today's a new day. Let's do this thing! We can do anything.

I made two calls. The first, to my plumber friend, Shawn, and the second to my dear friend, Marie. In addition to being very resourceful herself, Marie knows exactly how to talk me off the ledge. And boy was I on the ledge when I opened the "fucking bathroom" door again.

"Take pictures and send them to me," they both said. I sent the photos and waited as patiently as I could for each of them to get back to me. Shawn called first and explained the layout of the flange and in which direction to slide each johnny bolt to extract them from their keyhole slots. He reassured me that, "You've got this!"

Marie talked with *her* plumber friend, who coincidentally is also named Shawn. She also provided the in-person coaching and moral support I needed to get the old fasteners out and the new ones in. To say I was a little edgy during the entire johnny-bolt process would have been an understatement. I learned early on in life how to catastrophize just about everything. Anything in fact. My fear about something going terribly wrong at this point caused me to behave like a real jerk. Thankfully, Marie's calming and nurturing nature oozed out and filled the tiny room like a drug. I managed to settle down as if I had been gassed.

Once the longer spindles were in place, the rest of the toilet mounting process was comfortable, easy, and familiar. After the new wax seal was centered on the flange, I bear-hugged and lifted my toilet bowl into place. With the project nearing completion and my fear and anxiety starting to abate, I sat on the closed lid. Playfully, I wiggled my rear end around to help set the seal. The water supply hose was reconnected to the toilet's tank; then, the water valve was turned back on.

We waited patiently for the tank to fill. I felt around for leaks and found none. "We're doing good…this has been a long time coming", I said as I flushed. Once again, I felt around for leaks and found the floor dry!

"Halle freakin' lujah! I can *finally* shop for the effin' carpet now!

I thanked Marie and called it a day.

I'll shop for the carpet tomorrow. For today, it's progress not perfection.

Chapter 19

The Fidgeting Finish Line

Finally!
Today's the day I'm going to pick out new carpet! It's been a LONNNNG time coming.

***

I decided to try a local flooring company this time. No big billboards, fancy advertisements, or TV commercials with BS price promises. No well-dressed sales ladies with noisy shoes and closed body language either.

It's just a carpet after all.

***

Adjacent to a small and simple sales floor was a larger warehouse. The young woman who greeted me had visible tattoos and wore a stained shirt and welcoming smile. *Oh, thank God, somebody normal.* "Listen, my last encounter trying to do this didn't end so well, and it's been a very long road for me and this project. If I seem a bit short, please understand it's not you".

She listened politely and nodded appropriately as I recapped the previous shopping experience. "I'd really like to wrap this up before the heat of the summer kicks in". Once again overwhelmed by the variety of options, colors and textures, I left the store with a few samples and the determination to make a timely decision. I leaned into my discomfort.

It's just a carpet after all.

Eventually, I settled on "Spooky". In addition to being one of my cat's names, it presented as a nice, mottled color in the gray family. I wanted something neutral that was darker than what I had before—but not too dark. The mottling would be a nice change with a bonus benefit of camouflaging any future stains. I returned to the store, anxious to negotiate price and set up an installation date.

Having previously had the *bad* shopping experience

taught me that even carpet installation has parts that are negotiable. I felt confident that we would get the details completed on this visit. I could actually *see* the finish line waving excitedly in the wind.

"Hey, good to see you again. I've decided on Spooky. Let's get this scheduled", I said, practically skipping into the showroom.

Smiling, she responded, "Not so fast…we have to get our guy out there to do the official measurements."

I saw a bunch of guys milling about in the warehouse when I parked the car. My assumption was that one of them would come out to measure…maybe even follow me home right now and do it. Right?

"How long does that take"?

She smiled again. "Let me check when he's going to be in the area again. Oh, this darn computer…so slow".

"Your guys don't do the measuring"?

"No, we contract that part out…ok, I put you in…somebody *should* be calling you in a few days."

Feeling deflated, I responded weakly, "OK…I'll wait for the call".

For fucks sake, the finish line keeps fidgeting!
What am I not seeing?

Chapter 20
I'm Here Now

I *saw* the puke stains and the raised and shredded carpet loops from the cats. I *saw* the route most frequently taken across the carpet. I *felt* the strain of the seam tape trying desperately to hold the two sides together. I *know* this project has been a lesson in patience. I was beginning to feel defeated with each delay, snafu, hiccup, speed bump. I ran out of words. Force wasn't working; patience wasn't working. What now?

I surrender. I give up.

***

As soon as I loosened my grip and expectations, things moved quickly. I managed the new triggers of having strangers in my house like a champ. The old carpet was removed, the dusty floor beneath cleaned, and the new padding and carpet put in place! Aside from a broken outlet cover, the guys' work was clean and efficient. Hallelujah!

Oh, thank God it's done!

As soon as the guys left, I called a friend. "How's it look"?

"OKAY."

"Okay"? she repeated, questioning.

"Yeah, just ok".

***

I didn't have nearly the same excitement or pride as when the luxurious light gray carpet was first installed all those years ago. I felt icky...almost disconnected from myself. Weird. Unsettled. I forced myself to get on with my day. Every so often, I would stand in the kitchen and look at the new carpet in the big living room, questioning. *Wtf?*

Finally, I had an answer *and* overdue emotional eruption. The carpet that held so many memories was cut up, bound with duct tape, and discarded. All the love and laughter of the children who made me a great aunt, the friends and lovers who had passed through my life, the cats who were no longer in body…all of it that was captured in that carpet, was tossed away effortlessly, like a wadded-up old tissue carrying a chewed-up chunk of gum that lost its flavor.

I relate to that carpet... and the tissue.

***

I allowed myself the space and grace to grieve. I am becoming my own loving parent after all. Feeling somewhat relieved, I went on about my day until the next fiasco restarted my waterworks. The toilet in the half bath. You know the one. The wax seal had a meltdown of its own. Its failure caused a cascade of shit-brown water onto my paper products stored in the basement below. And I was beside myself; again, in tears.

In that precise moment, my wounded inner child was in the driver's seat, and things appeared catastrophic and out of control. *Why does this keep happening to me? Why? WHY? WHY!!!!??* In the short silence between sobs, I clearly heard this new voice for the first time. *This time*, it wasn't forced or wishful thinking; *this time*, it was crystal clear.

"Settle down, Sweetie, I'm here".

I froze.

The tears stopped, and my body instantly relaxed. In my mind's eye, I could see the wounded child in me backing up from the situation and settling down. Bewildered, and curious.

"I'm here now; let's do this together."

Chapter 21

The Voice

I'm here now; let's do this together.

***

Soft, gentle and reassuring, the voice was that of my inner loving parent. It is the voice fellow travelers in Adult Children of Alcoholics meetings talk about, the one I mistakenly *thought* I heard before. It was the voice absent from my childhood, and my parents', and theirs before them into the multi-generational abyss. I *knew* this was "the voice" because my body responded in a very peculiar way; it relaxed. I began to notice the voice as the loving, encouraging, and uplifting one. It was distinctly different from the voice that held my thoughts and observations. It was also entirely different from the brow-beating, inner critical parent I was most familiar with.

Take a breath. Easy now. One step at a time. We can do this… together.

Once settled, I realized that what I initially thought was shit water was actually rust water—not great, but thankfully no longer gag-worthy at least.

I really don't know how plumbers do this—even I wouldn't want to clean up my own shit water. Thank God it's not that.

Let's focus on the small victories and see what we can do.

The voice was right. A call to my plumber was promptly returned, and a thicker wax seal solved the leak later that day. It wasn't that catastrophic after all. The next day, a friend called to check on me. "So, how's the carpet look today…now that the toilet's fixed"? Once again, I found myself standing at the threshold between rooms searching for an answer. It was as if I was yelling "helllllllloooooo" into a canyon waiting for the response. Finally, I uttered, "it's blank…empty…bare…it's just a carpet".

***

My human senses were all activated. I saw the new carpet with my eyes and felt the fresh fibers under my bare feet. Inhaling the scent was delicious. I had felt my patience tested with nearly every step of the project. I recoiled when delays caused my inner critical parent to bash and browbeat me. I relived the memories, the love, the loss, the grief of years and years of tears, and fears, and laughter, and pain.

When the project appeared "done," I also finally *heard* my inner loving parent's soothing voice.

Yes, Sweetie, the carpet's done…but the real project has just begun.

Chapter 22
Real Project

Real project? Huh?

I spent time thinking about the chapters I had started to refer to the women in my writers' group as "the carpet series." What I initially believed was going to be a chapter or two about a never-ending house project turned out to be breadcrumbs leading me to my *real* project. A project of deep inner healing and eventually, peace.

***

No carpet. *A luxury we couldn't afford.*

Dirty, dog-hair-bound carpet with tangled gold tassels. Not being able to silence the voice of my overbearing and now long-dead grandmother shouting at my much younger self, "You're a terrible daughter! You disrespected your mother and treated her like trash!"

Hearing the thunk of Muffin's body connecting with the back of the closet after being drop-kicked into it.

Muffin's yipe.

Having my writer's group ask why I glossed over the first molestation that occurred shortly *after* the pup was punted like a football. Instinctively instantly answering with, "Because this is the carpet series…I'll get to that later," while secretly asking myself, "Why *did* I gloss over it? Is that the real reason?"

The flying pee pot. Angry shouting. Being *over* punished…Often.

Biting fleas. The smell of dog piss. More molestation.

Finding my mother dead.

Feeling alone and unwanted. Fending for myself.

***

This was my childhood.
This was my normal.

***

*Any **one** of these events would have been a lot for a child. Any **one** of them.*

With upgraded padding, strong seam tape, and fresh stain fighter in place, my new carpet has lovingly looped me into my latest truth.

Recovering myself *IS* my real project.

Chapter 23
Sweet 16

September 22, 2024

The girls I protected from a chronic child molester turned Sweet 16 today. When their mother was first presented with the information that her father repeatedly molested me as a child, she responded with a snarky denial of, "Yeah, well, people change." *She* wanted the perfect family: no drama, no crazy, no problems, no LGBTQIA, no dysfunction. *I* wanted to break the cycle and prevent history from repeating itself, to do what no one did for me-keep the twins safe and innocent as long as possible.

Their milestone birthday affected me deeply. My insides were overflowing with a multitude of polarizing emotions. Each feeling was fighting for attention, and my body responded accordingly. Fond memories brought warmth and relaxation. Not so fond memories caused tension, tightness, heaviness, and restriction. As a loving act of kindness and selfcare, I took myself for a bike ride and barefoot walk on the beach. Movement was important for processing all that arose for healing that day.

***

Sixteen.
Where was I when I was their age?

***

Smoking, drinking, and working at the local roller rink with one of my former abusers, the twin girls' maternal grandfather. Attending high school, playing recreational softball…secretly hating myself. Pretending. Lying. And grateful. I was extremely grateful that this abuser had moved on to other girls…prettier girls. Barbara, the taller, wavy-haired blonde who skated couples really well. Michelle, the short, dark-haired chick that easily weaved in and out as she sped past the other skaters.

Everybody saw him sucking face with his hands all over the blossoming teens. They were in full view, right there at the entry door. It wasn't done in secret like with me, and his sister, and countless others. His cocky, untouchable boldness was disgusting and turned my stomach. But it wasn't always that way.

***

He was a likeable guy, and people really enjoyed being around him. Neighborhood kids flocked to the house for the chance to learn how to box. Teaching drew us in. The attention we weren't getting anywhere else kept us coming back. It felt good. He made us each feel special. Special, just to him. Loyal, just to him. Being so enamored kept us quiet.

My first molester was like that too. He was friendly, helpful, handy, and smelled good after a shower. I learned how to care for hand tools, change a tire, and detail a car from him. During the grooming phase he also taught me how to properly make tuna salad. While leaning into me from behind, he demonstrated how to use the edge of a fork to push and drag the tuna chunk into much smaller threads. He explained how that was done *before* adding celery, onions and mayo. Unlike everyone else during that time, he was patient with me and incredibly kind.

Life back then put me in the company of one or the other future predators on a very regular basis. The time, attention, and learned skills during grooming were awesome. I felt special and appreciated. Seen and secretly adored.

***

*Why did I gloss over the molestation and reflexively defend what I wrote to my writer's group? What **was** going on back then?*

Present day me immediately felt a familiar tension in my body. Then panic. Then fear. I observed my sympathetic nervous system going into overdrive. The conscious awareness of my body's reactions caused my inner loving parent to take the wheel.

You're safe, Sherri. We're safe.

It's ok to feel it. I'm here.

Let it go.

Truth tears flowed. These were not the kind of tears that caused more pain. They were an acknowledgement of the courage it has taken to truly listen to my body's signals and the way it feels to heal.

I felt a burning lump in my throat. Instinctively. I *knew* it was from all the stifled childhood words, emotions, and wildly inappropriate experiences I was threatened to keep secret. Audible gurgling from my gut surfaced swiftly, then nausea. As I sat in my garage writing this chapter, I observed my body reacting to a legacy loop of a lifetime of undigested trauma. I *finally* had a space safe enough for it to be exorcised...*and* the courage to actually acknowledge and feel all the awful abuse.

They can't hurt us anymore. It wasn't right, and we didn't deserve or ask for any of it. None of it.

Holy shit, I gotta puke.

Through tears, I explosively wretched my morning coffee into a nearby garbage can.

After a few purposeful deep cleansing breaths, I blew my nose, wiped my face with my hand, and continued to write. Putting the words on paper and feeling my way through the process thwarted the throat pain. The tears, tension, and gut gurling were gone. With my appetite and sense of well-being restored, I felt lighter and ready to take on some more.

What was going on back then?

Chapter 24
Untangling the Twisted Truth

What's next, Sherri? Where do we go next? Do we finish up the carpet series or explore the molestation more?

***

The twisted truth is that I had multiple traumas twisting through my childhood simultaneously *and* at an alarming rate. I was terrified and felt unsafe more than any kid should *ever* have to feel even once. Alcoholic parents, psycho sibling, uptight grandmother, and two perverted predators prepping to pounce. As I prepared to write this chapter, I tuned into my body. Muscles tensed, breathing became shallow, and my heart rate rose. I also noticed that it is nowhere near as intense as it was just a few weeks ago. For that, I am thankful and hopeful.

***

In my mind's eye, I brought myself back to the apartment and moment when Muffin was drop-kicked. I imagined myself an observer, standing out of harm's way in the wide doorway between the living room and dining room. From this position, witness me was diagonal to the closet and entry door. The frame I saw was frozen like a movie. My mother's boyfriend was standing in front of the open closet door. My mother was to his right at the base of the wooden stairs that led up to the bathroom and second-floor bedrooms. What I found curious was that I saw a much younger girl, smaller than the age I actually was then. She was terrified and cowering behind her mother while tightly gripping the back of her shirt. And Muffin was out of view in the closet.

I have to be good. Don't ever make him mad. I have to be good. Don't ever make him mad.

Try as I might, I could *not* move that moment forward. I could not recall what happened next. When I first revisited that vision as my younger self, my body instantly reacted with the same terror and fear imprinted on me some fifty years ago. As an adult, I was able to recognize the irony and insanity of it all. I was clinging to my alcoholic and abusive mother, trying to hide behind her for safety. I saw little me and felt her fright. In that frozen frame, she was forced to stay close to the lesser of two evils.

*Was that much younger child actually **me** tied to a previous trauma? Or was I intuiting generational trauma as I clung to my mother?*

It was one of many "aha" moments as I untangled the twisted truth of my childhood *and* a starting place to unpack the shame I've carried for so long.

Chapter 25

Setting the Shame Aflame

Shame.

On the energetic vibration scale, shame is the lowest living frequency. It is just above death. I have been intimately familiar with shame for much, if not most, of my life. To heal, I had to start there. I had to make peace with the fact that so much of what I experienced was *not* my fault. It was never my fault. And I didn't deserve, or ask for, any of it.

***

They had been out drinking.

My mother and her boyfriend returned home after I was sound asleep. She was passed out drunk somewhere in the apartment, and *he* climbed into my bed. He was shirtless and wore boxers and the smell of scotch. Quietly, he slipped in between the sheets on the left side of my bed. At that time, my bed's headboard was on the far wall, facing the door.

What's happening? Why is Jack in my bed? What is he doing? Am I going to get in trouble?

I found myself in *my* bed with a man who had recently drop-kicked a helpless puppy into a closet, and my mother was out cold. Soon, my own mouth was filled with the taste of scotch, without having taken a sip. He was warm and gentle and touched me in places no one else had. Next, he took my right wrist and led my hand through the front slit of his boxers. Jack assisted me in the exploration of his manhood. And the scene goes blank.

I can't recall any more of that night. I know that what I *do* remember is more than enough for a little girl barely ten years old.

***

"Did you have fun last night"? he asked when he knew my mother was out of range.

Huh? Oh my God! That really did happen. Be good, Sherri. Don't ever make him mad.

I have no recollection of how, or if, I answered.

***

That was how it began with my mother's boyfriend. There were dozens of encounters in that apartment. I can easily replay flashes of sexual encounters in the shower, in my bedroom, in their bedroom, in the kitchen, and in his car. Intercourse was attempted often but not achieved because he could not maintain an erection. Orgasm and ejaculation were achieved through oral and manual methods. Eventually, the three of us moved from that apartment into the house funded by my grandmother's down payment. I remember one particular day when we were both running around the house naked when my grandmother showed up for a visit. I recall Jack hightailing his bare ass into the bedroom he shared with my mother after nervously saying, "Your grandmother's here…hurry up…get dressed"! And saying, "Wow…that was a close one!" after she left. Eventually, he and my mother broke up for good, and I never saw him again. Many years later, I experienced jolts of PTSD, grief, remorse, and shame when I stumbled on his obituary in the local paper.

***

Illegal and inappropriate sexual engagement with my second molester, the roller-skating Romeo from chapter 23, was a completely different experience. His manhood was always big and hard. Often, he'd thrust it up against me and erotically eye my expressions. Other times, he would force himself onto me and moan as he smelled the hair on the back of my head. Clothed or unclothed. It didn't matter. For him, it was a perverted power play. I can recall frequent incidents of being grabbed from behind with one arm, his free hand then jammed down my pants while his unit gyrated on my backside, getting his jollies off and forcing me to climax. He would snidely "celebrate" his success by sniffing his fingers and rubbing my scent on his upper lip. Later, he would scrunch his top lip up under his nose so he could smell me over and over again. His evil and condescending grin revealed that he was in complete control. There was nothing gentle about it, and there was nothing subtle about his boldness. His frequency and urgency were insatiable. Often, his libido found satisfaction with me in the basement, car, outside, and even in a bed with a person sleeping in between us. His then newborn baby was in a crib in the same room! Vividly, I recalled his arm under the person in the middle with his hand inappropriately inside my pajama bottoms. When I tried rolling away onto my side, he forcefully pulled me back and continued fingering my feminine folds.

I cannot recall the first or last experiences with this pompous, perverted predator—only the in between. I can only reason that it's because I was operating in shock and survival mode from Muffin being drop-kicked and the molestation with Jack that followed soon after. To add to the shame I carried, these molesters overlapped! I was never far from either one of them for several years. Not long before all of *this* trauma, I also suffered the loss of my dear grandfather. It's no wonder I had serious trust issues and turned to smoking and drinking as a teen.

***

Suffocating shame and fear mummified me and kept the details of these men's disgusting secrets for a long time—nearly fifty years in fact. All that shame and fear also kept me trapped from myself. With the shame set aflame and fear in the clear, true healing is finally here!

*The loss of my grandfather is described in my second book, "Unraveled: From Sibling Abuse to Sacred Self."

Chapter 26
I'm It

Nobody's coming.
Nobody is coming to save me.
To protect me.
To free me from living in fear.
To wipe my tears and make all the emotional pain and despair disappear.
Nobody's coming.
To be accountable.
To apologize.
To make up for what I got that I didn't deserve.
To love, care, and try to understand me.
Nobody.
I've finally accepted reality.
I'm it.

***

Once the carpet capers were compiled and the main molestations memorialized—yes, there were others. I placed my cupped hand over my mouth and gasped in horror. Reflexively, I noticed I was also holding my breath.

Oh my God!

My family was *that* family.

The family with a bunch of dirty secrets.

***

I realized that any *one* of those incidents would have been more than enough for a lonely little girl to experience. Any *one*. To review and revisit each of them took an enormous amount of inner strength, courage, and determination. The process was physically and emotionally exhausting. Intellectually, I knew my parents were alcoholics and my sibling abusive, but tuning in to the totality of the toxic toll that had taken on me took time.

***

Patience was paramount as I moved through each incident. The goal was to reframe them in a way that I could reach a sense of internal peace. It was important to connect with the frightened little girl hiding inside of me who was emotionally frozen in time. Working to gain her trust was essential to my sustained success and healing.

Ironically, the techniques I've used with abandoned, abused, and neglected animals proved useful in working with my seriously wounded inner child. For instance, the way I initially sat with Frankie, the vicious and unpredictable pit bull I wrote about in my first book, was the way I first sat with piss pot Sherri at the top of the stairs. Several times a week, I would mentally and intentionally "visit" that space in my memory. I would imagine my adult self, sitting near my younger self, on the crappily carpeted stairs as she held the handle of the soup pot thrown up the staircase at her. I sat and I sat. Lovingly. Consistently. I assured the traumatized little me that adult me wasn't going anywhere. As with Frankie, I took measured time to get closer and build trust with seriously wounded little Sherri. "I'll be back; we can talk when you're ready." Eventually, her eyes and rigid body softened. Surprisingly, I could feel the tension also leaving my adult body. I'd move closer. Sometimes, I would touch her shoulder or give her a kiss on the forehead before I left. Other times, I instinctively knew she was feeling prickly and ugly and didn't feel worthy of loving touch. I honored and respected her process. "Why?" she finally asked me. "Why is she so angry?" "What's wrong with me?" "Why can't I just use the bathroom?"

"Come with me," my inner loving parent said. "You're safe now…I won't let anyone hurt you anymore." I imagined offering my hand for safety, walking her down the stairs, and leading her to the bathroom like a big girl. I assured little me that I would guard the door.

My younger self emerged from the bathroom feeling relieved, safe, and secure. She also felt something every child should consistently feel; she felt loved. She shared a smile and enthusiastically reached for my hand. We took ourselves on a play date and rode the healing wave. While riding high and feeling good and supported I asked my younger self, "Is there some way we can reframe the experience of being angrily forced to pee in a pot useful?" Playfully and without skipping a beat, my inner little responded, "It already has…it's prepared us for a lifetime of peeing in the woods!"

Chapter 27
Shituations

"No no no NO NO! Please NO! Don't go over...don't go over...

DON'T!

GO!

OVER!"

I stood like a statue and stared at the spinning shit in the half bath toilet as the brown water rose rapidly. It was feverishly faster than I'd ever seen. Shocked and stunned by the sight, I was both frozen and mesmerized as I watched idly, waiting for it to stop. The scene seemed to stream far longer than I ever fathomed for a flushing floater.

"Please, please, please...NO!"

The water filling the tank for the next flush waned and the spiraling stool finally slowed to a stop. The murky water had risen as close as it possibly could have without going over. Not much more than a hearty spit would have pushed it beyond the border of the bowl.

"Thank you! Thank you! Thank you!"

I closed the lid and shut off the water. Turning it off was silly because I knew the toilet's tank was full and flush ready. I did it anyway and shushed the critical parent's voice in my head. Closing the bathroom door was equally ridiculous because the cats weren't going to push the handle down either. Catastrophizing convinced me that my main line had a major block; I was afraid to run *any* water for fear of causing a mucky mess. I took to brushing my teeth in the driveway with a bottle of water...just as if I were camping.

Fuck...now what? This toilet has NEVER clogged...the waste pipe below goes straight down and then over. In thirty-four years, this toilet has NEVER done THIS...NEVER.

A call to my regular plumber went straight to voice mail. I called a second and upon explaining my "shituation" was advised to contact a drain and sewer company instead. A quick search online had me consciously by-passing the most well-known contractor and choosing the second. As luck would have it, they were running a special, *and* the technician could be here within two hours! Sold!

Interestingly enough, instead of focusing on worst case scenarios and the shame of having to rely on a stranger to get me out of my crappy shituation, I called program friends for support and stayed present in my thoughts. What a refreshing change for me! I was adulting! Feeling relieved and encouraged, I focused on what I could do for myself right now.

***

I know I'm a great manifester and know how to manifest empty seats on airplanes and good parking spots. What kind of sewer technician do I want?

Send me a nice guy...send me a nice guy...send me a nice guy...and make sure he's competent.

Right on time! A clean and very new van arrived with a guy who immediately gave off a warm and friendly vibe. He was professional AND had a good sense of humor. After reviewing what might happen and additional costs associated with possible worst-case scenarios, I signed a release, and he got to work. Much to my own surprise, I was calmer than I had ever been in the past with this type of emergency. We chatted about his two French bull dogs for longer than it took him to snake my toilet.

Once it was all over, I realized that the last two years of actively working an ACA program are helping. I was able to revisit extremely dysregulating experiences that were trapped in my body and finally make peace with them.

The first happened at my maternal grandmother's house. I was young, maybe seven or eight years old. Her bathroom was off the dark dining room with the dirty carpet referred to in an earlier chapter. To the right of the dining room was a living room where others were gathered. Flushing the ancient toilet, which was seated next to the enormous and incredibly scary claw footed tub, resulted in the banging and clanging of old pipes. The water and waste remnants in the toilet rose and went over. I got scared. Really, really scared. I tried to escape the room with the angry steam radiator, uneven, soft linoleum tiled floor, banging pipes, and overflowing toilet only to realize the lock was jammed. I instinctively hesitated screaming for help because I *knew* this was somehow going to be my fault, and I would be beaten for it. Try as I might, I couldn't get out.

The lock was an early-generation dead bolt that had no business being installed on a bathroom door in the first place! I was trapped and had to yell for help. Eventually, one of my grandmother's adult foster kids climbed in through the window to release me. Even though I was totally terrified being held prisoner in the creepy bathroom, I am convinced that the delay releasing me lessened the severity of the unwarranted beating I received from my mother.

Two other major incidents happened at my mother's house. In the first, I was a teen home alone, waiting for the drain cleaner guy; our main sewer line was definitely clogged. Part of the clog was due to tree roots, the other tampons. Of course they couldn't be my mother's tampons, or both of our tampons, they were solely mine; I was accused of using too many. As if there were any possible way to truly tell whose was whose. In this instance, I watched in horror as the guy removed the cap from the sewer pipe in the basement, and everything that was stuck in there was encouraged to spill out onto the basement floor. It stank worse than anything I'd ever smelled before and was equally disgusting and disturbing. When the dude was done, he put the cap back on the sewer pipe and left me with the instructions to, "just spread some lime over it and sweep it up in a few days when it's dry."

Are you fucking kidding me? You're leaving me with this big mess AND having to tell a mother that comes home from work angry on a "good" day?

During the second, I was in my early twenties and there would definitely be no beating because mom was already dead and buried. Things were complicated because my grandmother didn't want my sibling and me to sell our mother's house. The house for which *she* funded the downpayment and therefore felt she had a voice in the house's disposition. My useless and helpless feigning sibling thought we could rent the place and become millionaires without having to lift a finger in its upkeep or maintenance. At the time, I lived with a friend, and my animals lived at mom's house. I'd go there a few times a day to care for them and check on things. One day, I smelled heating oil as soon as I crossed the threshold. My heart began thumping wildly, and extreme panic set in. I recall thinking that even turning on a light could cause the whole house to go Kaboom…killing me and my animals.

I have to act fast. Quick…shut off the furnace emergency switch!

I ping ponged back and forth between my thoughts that day and today…

What twenty-year-old today even knows what that is? Much less a twenty-year-old girl. And how the hell did I even know to do that? We are amazing problem solvers.

I hit the emergency switch and took a breath.

What next?

A flashlight.

I spoke to myself as if I weren't alone…as if there were more than one of me or I had the support of someone else close by.

Let's get a flashlight so we can go downstairs safely and not blow up the entire neighborhood.

Cautiously, I descended the basement stairs. The smell of heating oil intensified. My heart pounded so loudly I thought for sure the neighbors could hear it too. When I got to the bottom of the stairs, I rounded the corner and flashed the light in the direction of the antiquated heating unit. In nearly the same area as the sewage sat years before, fuel oil was pooled.

Fuck…what a mess!

Gotta call Gramma and the heating guy.

Turns out, something in the unit had failed and needed to be replaced. Cleanup was going to be similar to the sewage mess, left up to me. This time Speedy-dry, a product closely related to cat litter, was spread over the spill. It could be swept up once the oil was absorbed.

As terrifying as these incidents were for me in the

moment, I have two key takeaways today. The first is that I should have *never* had to deal with them alone. Never. No kid should have ever had to endure or be solely responsible for what I was. The second is the realization that because of the crazy shituations I was put in as a youngster, I have absolutely amazing problem-solving skills…and for that, I am grateful.

Chapter 28
Loved Unconditionally

November 19, 2024

The sound startled me.

I instinctively stopped breathing.

To keep myself safe…I had to be quiet.

I held my breath as long as I could before taking the shallowest and quietest one I could possibly muster. There it was again. I fidgeted uncomfortably. Terrified. *What is that?* Again, I held my breath and listened closely. I tried to remain as still as possible. My long-forgotten childhood fear of the dark had officially returned with a vengeance, complete with all the physical sensations of imminent danger.

***

It started with incessant coughing late the night before. Fatigue set in, and the next day was spent between the couch and the futon. Sometimes I watched the TV and sometimes, the TV watched me. I eventually gave up and put myself to bed. In the quiet darkness, I heard a young child whining slightly louder than a whisper. It startled me. Deeply. The wheezing in my chest on exhale mimicked a sad, lonely child needing comfort and loving care. The sound, a sound I would get beaten for making as a child, triggered many memories.

The words, "I was not allowed to be sick," rang in my head in different voices, my own at different ages and in the voices of others who once meant the world to me. In between wheezes, I did my best to comfort the sick little girl who was never *allowed* to be sick. The sick little girl who had to soldier through any ailment lest she be beaten by her mother or ridiculed and mocked to tears by her elder sibling. Sometimes both. On this night, I mustered the strength to put the memories of others on the shelf. It was high time I practiced being present for my younger self.

Lovingly, I rubbed Vick's on her chest and under her

nostrils. I imagined snuggling close to little me with one of the last gifts I received from the twins I mentioned in a previous chapter...their innocent young voices still fresh in my head. *Here, Aunt Sherri, this is from us because everybody needs a fuzzy pink princess blanket.* I coughed a few more times before clearing the whining wheeze for the night and drifting off peacefully to sleep.

There was more couch and channel surfing on Wednesday in addition to the memory parade of children, friends, family members, lovers, and others whom I'd cared for during illnesses. Some of the memories were warm and loving, and others left me shaking my head as to why I was the one doing the caregiving.

How do I know how to love and nurture when I have NO memories of ever receiving that type of treatment as a child?

Surrendering to my feelings, I sobbed uncontrollably. I thought about what it was like to be sick as a child and grieved for my younger self. I recalled my mother's looks of disgust and apathy. And my elder sibling's taunting words, "Aw...look at the little crybaby...poor Sherri".

How dare I get sick and require loving care and attention? How dare I?

I allowed myself to feel it—all of it: sick, sad, needy, helpless. It took effort to steer my thoughts away from all the others. I worked hard and kept the focus on my own needs in the moment. Eventually, I felt a loving presence stirring inside. I've come to know this being as my inner loving parent—the one I never had growing up. The voice helped reign in my thoughts and reminded me that everybody gets sick sometimes. And that's okay. Feelings of a deep, unconditional love washed over me. The whining ceased. I drifted off to sleep feeling safe, secure.

And loved unconditionally.

Chapter 29
Fuckin' A

December 2024

I started this December with a deep sigh.

Fuckin' A, here it is again. Already. Come onnnnnn December 26ᵗʰ!

***

"Fuckin' A."

Literally, one of the last intelligible words a dear friend of mine ever muttered to me. It wasn't my favorite catch phase. It was hers. Yet here it was in my head. Hearing the phrase transported me back to that time. She was in hospice, and I would visit often—she was terminal. Our earlier conversations were two-way with each of us taking turns "catching up." Over time, they became one-way with me talking, reminiscing or storytelling and her responding with, "Fuckin' A," as a way to participate. At some point, her responses deteriorated to single-syllable grunts or mmm's shortly before she was unable to respond verbally at all. Undeniably, "Fuckin' A", was her favorite catch phrase and said often in my company—many times with an accompanying head shake or eye roll for effect. I would smile or laugh every single time she said it. Hearing it again during the start of another agonizing holiday season made me go inward.

***

It doesn't feel good to be wishing my time away.

I have an army of friends that have gone before me…and others with families and small children that are struggling with sickness. It doesn't feel good to rush through my time on earth.

How can I do December and the "Horror-day" season differently this year?

Why is my dead Fuckin' A friend in my head?

***

Jackie, affectionately known by her close friends as "The Cookie Bitch" LOVED baking holiday cookies and preparing meals for others. In fact, she'd make lasagna with sausage and meatballs for her birthday every November…even though she didn't eat meat. Her kitchen creations weren't made from guilt and obligation. Oh no. *Her* food's binding agents were 100% pure love and appreciation. And, contrary to the lame lasagna in chapter one, hers was effing fantastic!

As an adoptee, Jackie knew how it felt to be abandoned by those first entrusted to love and protect her. She and I would often commiserate about how much we did for others and how they would show their gratitude by disappointing us over and over and over again. The people we gave more chances to than they ever deserved—hoping it would be better "this time." We were a good mirror for each other. And we would both give each other the advice we wouldn't take for ourselves. "Fuckin' A."

***

How can I do it differently?
How can I do it my way?
What does "my way" even look like?

***

I've come a long way since chapter 5! And…I can certainly see the complete circle, or legacy loop, that I created with the cookies and lasagna. With gentleness and honesty, I took time to reflect on what "worked" last December and what didn't. I knew I wasn't going to put up a tree or decorate, and I was totally good with that. Changing "Christmas Presents" into "Gratitude Gifts" helped reduce much of my gift giving angst this year as well. Baking new memories from chapter one was fun, and I'd be open to doing that again. I felt the same about building gingerbread houses, decorating ugly sweater cookies, the kids' holiday party at the Elk's, and the other activities too. It also felt incredible knowing I wouldn't be getting a guilt lunch invitation either since I terminated that unsafe friendship. What an amazing gift of gratitude…to myself!

Internally, I noticed that I felt neither obligated nor attached to any of it. *That* was a genuine healing moment for sure. With the exception of one emotional meltdown in early December, I was able to be truly present to each moment of every day before, during, and after Christmas. Some of the plans didn't work out, and I easily maintained my center and rolled with the changes. There were no silent storms inside myself. No external tantrums either. I immersed myself in holiday stuff and left when I'd had enough.

I adulted.

Thank you, Jackie. I'm finally taking our own advice.

Fuckin' A!

Chapter 30

Sink or Swim

When I think, I can sink.
When I feel, I can heal.

***

I lost another friend today.
To addiction.
Addiction caused by loneliness.
Loneliness in a room full of people.
People who couldn't see the pain.
The pain of their past.
Their past abuse and neglect.
Abuse and neglect that led to addiction for hope.
For hope to cope.
To cope with the shame and guilt.
The shame and guilt that kept us quiet.
Quiet lest we stir the pot.
The pot our abusers want the lid to stay on.

***

Many years ago, I slid the lid and let some shame and blame find the flame. The diseased marrow packed into the skeleton bones of my family's alcoholism and dysfunction required time and effort to break down. To simmer. To cool. Like a sizzling stove, the emotional pain was way too hot to touch at first. Slowly, I began to learn and acknowledge how the events of my childhood took a tremendous toll on my soul.

Like the friend mentioned above, and many others before him, I too shuffled around various addictions. I shuffled to cope. And hope. For better days. To be seen. Cared for. And loved. I continued to look outside myself for answers. To blame. It was the game. The game of shame.

***

I thought about my friend who died. I thought about what we had in common and where we differed. We grew up in the same neighborhood, attended the same schools, knew many of the same people, and had alternative lifestyles. He had many siblings and lived out of the country for a while. I only had one sibling and have not yet moved out of the state into which I was born. We were both abused and mistreated by our siblings, families, and others in positions of authority over us. One of us found recovery, and the other didn't.

In recovery, I'm learning how to actually feel my emotions instead of thinking about how I or others think I *should* feel. There is a distinct difference. Feeling means I'm healing.

When I *think* about feeling, I take myself out of experiencing life. Thinking had me trying to make sense of things that will never make sense. It kept me stuck in a legacy loop…asking questions to which there are no good answers. Why do people hurt others? Why do some find recovery while others languish?

Why?

Today, I know where *my* feelings end and someone else's begin. I can grieve the loss of my friend. I can also have empathy for the abusive childhood he suffered most of his life. I can synchronously feel compassion for my own pain and gratitude for the recovery I work daily to maintain.

***

When I think, I can sink.
When I feel, I can heal.

Chapter 31

Mottled Memories

It felt so real. Surreal.

So real. Surreal.

Mottled. Modeled.

Similarly sounding words get my attention. They are akin to crusty crumbs resting on the fringes of an old rag rug, just like the old rag rugs that marked the front and back doors to my childhood home. The childhood home I dreamt about last night…from a safe distance.

***

It felt so real. Surreal.

Mottled. Modeled.

I stand courageously on the fringes of deep healing through feeling.

Feeling the deep grief of a childhood mottled by that which was modeled.

***

I found myself dreaming. It was something I hadn't done in weeks. Maybe even months. Much of my deepest healing is done during the darkness of night. In current dreams, my emotions seem softer, and I feel safe to explore them in healthy ways. Last night's dream was one of those moments.

***

I stood in a roadway of concrete tracks with strangers. The lanes were simultaneously entangled and intersected. It was as if the spiraling exit of a parking deck and the loops of a Matchbox race car set were attempting to make a baby. The strangers and I stood on the north side of a small brook that looked up a short hill at my childhood home. The sloped, double driveway was empty. There sat a small orange car parked on the road to the left of the home's entrance. The front door was open, but the house appeared vacant.

"I used to live there." I mumbled to the strangers as I noticed myself drifting away. Drifting away from the people…drifting away from my thoughts. Knowing I was dreaming. Wanting to pay attention to what was being revealed to be healed. In my dream, I inched closer…closer to my childhood home.

At first, my feelings were mottled. I was a happy-go-lucky kid who enjoyed playing in the yard, sledding down the short hill in winter, and splashing around in the brook during the summer. In the fall, the neighbor kids and I would rake and jump in leaves or play nighttime hide and seek. I also remember making Snoopy snow cones on the porch and loving up on newborn kittens in our front yard. Those fun and fleeting moments occurred in the absence of my alcoholic parents and abusive sibling. I floated further from the strangers as I acknowledged a deep grief surge within my soul.

My dream began to connect with my waking life even though I was still in a deep sleep.

We need to call a program friend to talk through this unexpressed grief. We can't heal in isolation.

Effortlessly, I was connected to the person I last interacted with before falling asleep. In the continuation of the dream within a dream, I spoke to my fellow traveler in fragments, like a frightened child. I *knew* they were responding kindly, but I couldn't hear or absorb their words. It was as if my love receiver were broken. I couldn't hear or accept what was offered.

The conditional mottled modeling of love I was born into was being revealed to be healed! My friend's voice faded further. "I have to go…I have to go…I have to take care of my inner family." I said in my dream.

"Wait…just hold on…don't hang up…wait."

"I gotta go. I have to take care of myself. It's an inside job."

***

In the stillness of that moment, I heard the most important thing.

I LOVE YOU.

***

It feels so real. *Surreal.*

***

I LOVE YOU TOO.

Chapter 32

From Hell to Whole

Another hellacious memory surfaced today.

The memory spun like a stubborn stool skirting the perimeter of a toilet. It refused to surrender, change shape, or break apart into smaller, manageable pieces. The memory fought attempts to direct my thoughts elsewhere, just like a piece of spiraling shit fights the suctioning current of multiple flushes. It wouldn't go away! I had to write about it. I had to write about it because it was circling like a loop. A legacy loop.

We were in the next-door neighbor's finished basement. I remembered that the floor had the same tile as the hallways in the high school. Even though I was still a long way from attending high school, I instantly knew the tile was the same. The neighbor boy was there wearing his nose-taped, dirty, black, nerdy glasses, a stained, white, T-shirt, tighty-whitey underwear, and tube socks. My psycho sibling was there too.

"Let's play a game," my twisted sister said.

The neighbor boy, six years my senior, was lying on his back. His feet were on the floor, with knees bent and legs spread apart. I was forced between his legs in a way where our privates touched. Try as I might, I can't remember what, or if, I was wearing clothes. I also can't remember if the neighbor boy's sister was there or not. Once I was in position, I remember hearing laughter, a very dark and evil laughter.

This wasn't a game. It was a set up. A very disturbing set up.

"Either you tell Mommy what you just did, or I will."

"What did I do?"

"You f**ked Michael."

"Huh?"

***

I don't remember how old I was. I do know I was young, still in elementary school...my sibling, seven years older than I.

Up until that point, I don't think I'd ever even heard the "F" word, much less knew what it meant. And here I was, "doing it," long before I should have been.

Fear washed over me.

Again.

I froze. Deep in thought.

Which beating would be worse? The one I'd get if I told Mommy, or the one I'd get if she did?

No wonder this memory spun like shit. My choices were shitty and shittier!

I guess it's better if she hears it from me.

***

"Go ahead…if you don't tell her I will!"

***

I could hear the loud whir of the pale yellow, General Electric, steel cannister vacuum through the front screen door before I even opened it. It was spring cleaning time. The nozzle was sliding and clunking around on the hardwood floor inside the hall closet. The closet was near the wide entrance that led into the kitchen. Mother was sitting on the floor beside the vac, vigorously steering the head into each corner.

"Go ahead…tell her," I heard from behind.

Like the soft center of an innocent Oreo cookie, I found myself sandwiched between two equally evil women. Both made my life a living hell. One tortured and tormented me for sport, and the other beat the shit out of me for no good reason. And I couldn't do anything about it. Then.

Shaking with fear, my legs felt like rubber. Sheepishly, I approached.

"Ma." I waited for her to turn around. "I f**ed Michael."

In the silence of this moment, I can still hear that old vacuum's motor running. I can still see the look of complete confusion on my mother's face coupled with her question of, "Whaaaaat?" I hear my sibling's snickers behind me. I can taste the salt of my tears, knowing it wasn't going to get better anytime soon. And the memory stops swirling. I don't *know* what happened next. I don't *know* if she heard me, asked me to repeat it, beat the crap out of me, or if I just ran away crying.

***

I've read a lot about childhood development. I *know* there are innocent, exploratory, age-appropriate behaviors that occur between kids of similar ages. "You show me yours, and I'll show you mine." This was not that. This was also not an isolated incident.

My inner loving parent stepped forward for reassurance.

This was not your fault. And you did not deserve any of it. I am so sorry that happened to you and no one was there to protect you. I'm here now and will never leave you again.

I lived through hell.

Writing about and healing from my legacy loops is returning me to whole.

Chapter 33
Letting Go

Writing this book and honestly diving into the horrors of my childhood was a cake walk compared to the legacy looping lessons in letting go.

Some days, I still notice myself waking up with my jaw and fists clenched. Where is it stuck? Is it subconscious tension from not having a safe place to fully express myself growing up? From feeling constantly on guard to protect myself? Or is it my body's defense system...systematically preparing for the next blow? Or is it coming from some other part of me ready to finally fight back? On mornings like this, I summon my inner loving parent. She gently and lovingly steps forward to remind us we're safe.

They can't hurt us anymore. It's ok to relax. It's ok to feel. We are safe. I've got you.

On days with a physical response, selfcare is paramount, and gentleness is key. I slow everything down...pay close attention to my needs.

How do I feel?

What would feel good to me in this moment? What is the most loving thing I can do for myself right now?

Each day is different. I may find myself wanting a walk in nature, being around well-behaved kids or animals, yoga, massage, a bubble bath, movie, or fancy meal. Some days it's a midday nap, watching bad TV, writing, reading or an in-person ACA meeting. Maybe I no longer want to do that thing I previously committed to, or maybe I want to go balls to the wall and hike double-digit miles with or without a hiking buddy. I've invested a lot of time and effort into my physical recovery, and it feels good...even on the "bad" days. There are far fewer of them since undertaking this life-altering work! When I listen closely to what my body is saying, I am in a better position to let go of the tension.

Beliefs are another story. My abusive sibling repeatedly

called me ugly names, some of which have been permanently banned from the dictionary. Additionally, my caregivers treated me as if I were those ugly names and irrelevant. I truly believed I was lower and less-valuable than the lowest rung on a ladder—not even worthy of being stepped on so others could advance. So often, I felt like I had to prove myself worthy…worthy of love, attention, and respect that would never come. That behavior was exhausting as a child and even more so as the adult child I grew into. Today, I catch myself when the "less than" beliefs show up in my thoughts. Like a balloon loosely tied to a child's wrist, the false belief floats away when I recognize it's not my belief. It's craziness somebody else pinned to me long ago. If it's not mine to hold onto, I have become willing to let it go.

My fondness for freefalling feelings like bitterness, resentment, jealousy, anger, helplessness, frustration, and more was a legacy looped into my DNA pre-birth. Over time, those insatiable bloodsuckers siphoned the life out of me like thirsty ticks attack an innocent and unsuspecting host. Everyone *but me* saw them. Until I acknowledged these flailing feelings, they ate away at my soul. I was powerless to let go of what I didn't know was hurting me. Like a match to a tick, recovery fires my desire to let go of low-level longings.

People are another story. Some whom I've chosen, some who just showed up, those whom I wouldn't have chosen but got stuck with, and those whom I fought loving in the first place out of fear of abandonment. I'll start with family, many of whom I wouldn't have chosen but was stuck with. For over five decades, I believed that family was forever, blood was indeed thicker than water, and that *they* were my safety net. Those beliefs were in direct conflict with my childhood experience of torture, abuse, and neglect at the hands of family. My family wasn't safe, but they were also all I knew. My self-righteous, noble, inbred sense of loyalty to "the family" kept me returning to unhealthy others like a junked car to a scrap magnet. Looking back, I saw myself as the mole in a never-ending game of whack-a-mole. A perpetual victim.

I'll just try harder, do more…give more. They'll come around…they'll see my value.

It felt like an act of God would be necessary to break the invisible pull. I consciously clung to the crazy as if my life depended on it. As family members died off, I finally came to see that the firstborn, my one and only sibling, is and has been, our family's puppet master. They have strings attached to so many including offspring, grandkids, cousins, and unsuspecting others. Over time, their cords attached to *me* have frayed and disintegrated into dust. But others who were once a very large part of my life consciously choose to remain part of this person's destructive shit show. Some of "those" have been the hardest for me to let go of. "Those" who have said they don't want to get in the middle but whose umbilical cords jerk them back into place when they stray. There are others I've involuntarily had to let go of because evil and fear forced them into submission. It's been hard some days…really hard in fact because I never ever wanted to make them feel abandoned, especially by me. Never.

The folks that just showed up were mainly in the workforce and people I ran in similar circles with. Most of my former co-workers have been super easy to let go of. Many of them never even had a chance to make it into the friend column. I just won't do shallow and superficial anymore. I can't. There is no residual effect, no grieving process, and no wished bad luck or harm. It was a healthy type of letting go.

People I've gotten really close to are another story. They have been some of the hardest to let go. Whether taking a break from a friendship or permanently terminating ties, it's hard and just plain sucks. I never wanted to make others feel the way they made me feel. There are so many amazing memories that sneak in and give me ad interim amnesia as to why I stepped away in the first place. Sometimes, the memories make me want to "take the high road," reach out, reconnect, and try again. Before taking action, I hear my therapist's voice. It comes to me from behind a green, gold-fringed curtain like the great and powerful Oz. "When people show you who they are, believe them…the first time!" Next, I hear my inner child and inner teen's voices chime in. "We wanna play with people who show up when they say they gonna show up, do what they say they gonna do, don't ditch us for a better offer, and don't leave us hanging or guessing how important we are to them…because they consistently show and tell us!" Lastly, my inner loving parent steps forward, "When we right our relationship with ourselves first, the right relationships will come next…it's ok for us to let them go."

***

The hardest of all to let go of is the one I fought so hard to love in the first place, my greatest teacher. She was so full of love and abundant energy! Her love was given freely to every cause, every animal, every person…even those who mistreated, mocked, used, abused, and took advantage of her. She believed that her only value was to give, give, give. Kindness was the key she presented others. And being locked on having her own wants and needs met last was her prison. There was so much distance between us. How would this possibly work?

Let's take it slow.

I couldn't see what I couldn't see. That legacy loop played itself out in so many ways…reflexive responses of yes, people, places, things, food, snacks, songs, notes, scents, gifts, holidays, trinkets. The list of reminders and memories seems to go on forever.

It wasn't all bad. Maybe I can go back. I miss her…and the things left unfinished.

Letting go of that last one has been one of the most difficult, yet necessary, parts of my emotional recovery. My head knows it's both exhausting and fruitless to keep chasing unhealthy, period. Staying present and limiting my exposure to anyone who regularly engages in behaviors and activities I've worked incredibly hard to overcome *is* letting go. It's letting go of a lifelong legacy loop of feeling unworthy, unlovable, less than. My list of unhealthy coping strategies was long. It included different types of addiction, co-dependence, under-achieving, enmeshment, parasitic symbiosis, over-spending, under-spending, black-and-white thinking, people-pleasing, not allowing others to have their own feelings or make their own mistakes, running, over-busying myself and more. The very things that frustrated me about others were behaviors I previously engaged in.

Before recovery, I thought I *had* to agree with everyone or go to battle and fiercely argue my position. Today, instead of getting carried haphazardly downstream, I let go of discussions with a destination to nowhere. I love, love, love, exercising my "choice" muscles!

Continuing to love that last one...my greatest teacher...from a distance...is the most loving thing I can do. It's time to let her go and start loving ourselves...first.

"Change is hard," she acknowledges.

Staying stuck is harder.

Goodbye old me...it's time to let you go.

Epilogue

April 15, 2025

Back in the 1990's, as I was winding up my alcohol abuse and recovering from breast cancer, family dynamics expert John Bradshaw put American family dysfunction at 96%. Ninety-six percent! That figure includes teachers, doctors, nurses, therapists, clergy, and others in "helping" professions. No surprise since "people pleasing," having an "overdeveloped sense of responsibility," putting everyone else's needs first, lack of boundaries, and the inability to say "no" to others out of fear of being abandoned are classic traits of dysfunction. Those traits are also acceptable social signs of being "nice" and "successful."

Validated.

By the 96%.

Ninety-six percent of the American population was either doing things others told them to do, *doing* what they thought they *should do* to keep the peace and avoid conflict, *or* denying there were any problems at all. Ninety-six percent. I was one of them. It's no wonder I felt comfortable in chaos and crazy. I marinated in it.

Secretly, I was more relieved than scared by my mid-ninety's health diagnosis. I was relieved because *then* I had a built-in excuse for starting to say "no" without feeling guilty about it. "Sorry, I can't... I have a doctor's appointment, chemo, no energy..." Looking back, I realize how truly sick and dysfunctional my thinking was. I always felt like I had to answer others and explain or defend my "no." And that it had better be a "good" excuse. I believed my only value was in giving to others. Having enjoyed what, I perceived to be pretty good *physical* health into my thirties, the "giving" of my left breast was definitely my first "big" wake-up call. I began to develop an internal honesty with myself and paid more attention to how *I* felt, what *I* wanted, and what my body was trying to tell me. It would still take time to change, but at least I started to listen to myself. *"Progress Not Perfection."*

American society defines "success" by the size, not quality, of your circle. I carried the unspoken perception that my value was determined by invisible, outside sources. I felt defined by the size and location of my house, the importance of my profession, the cost of my car, *and* most importantly, my ability to conform…with the dysfunctional ninety-six percent! I was held captive to what I now call, "compare despair." Being completely oblivious to my own resilience, tenacity, courage, and strength kept me trying to please others and holding on to unhealthy beliefs about myself and unfulfilling relationships. It was exhausting on all levels.

Despite the noticeable rise in addictions, death by loneliness, suicide, cancer, heart-related deaths, and chronic pain, more than three decades later, Artificial Intelligence (AI) inquiries report family dysfunction between 70 to 80%. The percentage is crawling in the right direction because courageous people like me are choosing to break the family rules of, "Don't talk, don't trust, don't feel," through the telling of our stories.

I gather daily with other adult children to share my personal experiences, strength, and hope for an emotionally healthier existence. My recovery family understands and supports me in ways I've only ever dreamed. They certainly don't have all the answers or try to fix me. Instead, the group forms the life ring around my heart. They keep it safe and listen patiently as I work through the ebbs and flows of my sometimes-stormy emotional tides. The beauty is in watching how this often-times difficult, life-altering program calmly and lovingly ripples out as an encouraging life-line to others.

Through untangling my own legacy loops, I am healing me and healing you.

I Am Here

I AM
Here
To learn
Gentleness,
For Me
For You
For The World

I AM
Here
To teach
Gentleness,
For Me
For You
For The World

I AM
Here
To learn
Forgiveness
For Me
For You
For The World

I AM
Here
To teach
Forgiveness,
For Me
For You
For The World

I AM
Here
To learn

Love,
For Me
For You
For The World

I AM
Here
To teach
Love,
For Me
For You
For The World

I AM
LOVE
For Me
For You
For The World

Love Me
Love You
Love The World

You
Are Me

We
Are
One

Resources

The resources listed below represent the tools I've used to date in my healing journey.

Audio

Shianna Noll. (2009). *Songs for the inner child.* [Album]. Cairomy.

Books

ACA World Service Organization. (2023) *A new hope by ACA: ACA beginners' handbook (fellowship review mode).* Adult Children of Alcoholics/Dysfunctional Families.

ACA World Service Organization. (2006). *Adult children of alcoholics/dysfunctional families ACA fellowship text (The big red book).* Adult Children of Alcoholics/Dysfunctional Families.

ACA World Service Organization. (2013). *Strengthening my recovery: Meditations for adult children of alcoholics/dysfunctional families.* Adult Children of Alcoholics/Dysfunctional Families.

ACA World Service Organization. (2021). *The loving parent guidebook: The solution is to become your own loving parent).* Adult Children of Alcoholics/Dysfunctional Families.

Burmeister, A. with Monte, T. (1997). *The touch of healing: Energizing body, mind, and spirit with the art of Jin Shin Jyutsu.* Bantam Books.

Campbell, S. (2019). *But It's Your Family: Cutting ties with toxic family members and loving yourself in the aftermath.* Morgan James Publishing.

Coello, P. (1993). *The alchemist.* (T. Translator, Trans). Harper-San Francisco. (Original work published 1988).

Gibson, L. (2015). *Adult children of emotionally immature parents: How to heal from distant, rejecting, or self-involved parents.* New Harbinger Publications.

Heisler, T.W. (2023). *The shadow in our lives: One family's recovery from child sexual abuse.* Tracy Wilson Heisler.

Hendrix, H. & Hunt, H.L. (2019). *Getting the love you want: A guide for couples.* 3rd ed. St. Martin's Griffin.

Jaouad, S. (2022). *Between two kingdoms: A memoir of a life interrupted.* Random House Trace Paperbacks.

Lerner, H. (2014). *The dance of anger: A woman's guide to changing the patterns of intimate relationships.* Perennial Library.

Levine, A. & Heller, R. (2012). *Attached: The new science of adult attachment and how it can help you find and keep love.* Tarcher.

Maté, G. & Maté, D. (2022). *The myth of normal: Trauma, illness, & healing in a toxic culture.* Avery.

Myss, C. (2006). *Invisible acts of power: Channeling grace in your everyday life.* Atria Books.

Perry, B. D. & Szalavitz, M. (2017). *The boy who was raised as a dog and other stories from a child psychiatrist's notebook: What traumatized children can teach us about loss, love and healing.* Basic Books.

Real, T. & Springsteen, B. (2022). *US: Getting past you and me to build a more loving relationship.* Rodale Books.

Rogers, K. (2017). *Racing with my shadow: The compelling true story of America's first female jockey.* Create Space Independent Publishing Platform.

Sarno, J. E. (2007). *The divided mind: The epidemic of mindbody disorders.* Harper Perennial.

Sarno, J. E. (2007). *The mindbody prescription: Healing the body, healing the pain.* Warner Books, Inc.

Schwartz, R. C. (2021). *No bad parts: Healing trauma & restoring wholeness with the internal family systems model.* Sounds True.

Simms, M. (2023). *The secret lives of teeth: Understanding emotional influences on oral health.* Holistic Tooth Fairy, Ltd.

Tawwab, N. G. (2021). *Set boundaries, find peace: A guide to reclaiming yourself.* Tarcher.

Tawwab. N. G. (2021). *The set boundaries workbook.* Tarcher.

Terkeurst, L. (2022). *Good boundaries and goodbyes: Loving others without losing the best of who you are.* Thomas Nelson.

Whitfield, C. L. (1990). *A gift to myself.* Health Communications Inc.

Winfrey, O. & Perry, B. D. (2021). *What happened to you: Conversations on trauma, resilience, and healing.* Flatiron Books: An Oprah Book. (audio version)

Woititz, J. G. (2010). *Adult children of alcoholics expanded edition.* Health Communications Inc.

Woititz, J. G. (1986). *Struggle for Intimacy.* Health Communications Inc.

Woititz, J. G. & Garner, A. (1990). *Lifeskills for adult children.* Health Communications Inc.

Wolynn, M. (2017). *It didn't start with you: How inherited family trauma shapes who we are and how to end the cycle.* Penguin Life.

Zoffness, R. (2020). *The pain management workbook.* New Harbinger Publications

Free Publications

ACA World Service Organization. (1992). *25 questions.* https://adultchildren.org/wp-content/uploads/2024/06/25_Questions_EN_US_A4.pdf

ACA World Service Organization. (n.d.) *For the beginner.* *https://adultchildren.org/wp-content/uploads/2024/06/To_the_Beginner_EN_US_A4.pdf*

ACA World Service Organization. (1978). *Laundry list.* *https://adultchildren.org/wp-content/uploads/Literature/The_Laundry_List_EN-US_A4.pdf*

ACA World Service Organization. (2015). *Tool bag.* *https://adultchildren.org/wp-content/uploads/2024/06/The_Tool_Bag_EN_US_A4.pdf*

ACA World Service Organization. (2015). *What is ACA?.* *https://adultchildren.org/wp-content/uploads/2024/06/ACA_is_EN-US_A4.pdf*

Self-Care and Supportive Healing Practices
Bowen therapy also known as Bowenwork® or Bowtech

Color therapy

Epsom salt baths with lavender, rosemary or rose petals

Economy, D. (2025). *Holistic psychotherapy / constellation work.* *https://douglaseconomy.com/holistic%20psychotherapy-constellation%20work/*

Jin Shin Jyutsu®

Massage

Meditation

Pranic Healing

Reiki

Spending time outside in nature

Sound Therapy

Step into joy healing arts, llc. (n.d.) *Healing with horses.* *https://stepintojoyhealingarts.com/healing-with-horses/*

The center of being, inc. (2025). *Integrated energy therapy®. http://www.learniet.com*

Yoga

Video

Gabor Maté. (2023). *Abandonment trauma.* [Video]. YouTube. https://www.youtube.com/watch?v=P087SYOV6_I

Gabor Maté. (2023). *The childhood lie that's ruining all of our lives.* [Video]. YouTube.

https://www.youtube.com/watch?v=uPup-1pDepY

John Sarno (2017). *All the rage.* [Video]. Vimeo.

Mantak Chia. (2022). *Six healing sounds.* [Video]. YouTube. https://www.youtube.com/watch?v=M2Gs0plt0fE

Websites

ACA World Service Organization. (2023). *Welcome to adult children of alcoholics & dysfunctional families.* http://www.adultchildren.org

Acknowledgements

Without my writers' group riding shotgun, I could not have completed this work. Karen Hodges Miller, Wendy Wyatt, and Janice Detrie, I appreciate you more than words could ever express. Your loving support and attention to detail has allowed me to create an amazing book on a very sensitive subject.

Listing *everyone* who assisted with untangling the legacy loops that kept me captive in dysfunction would be nearly impossible. But here goes, in no particular order. As a grown adult, I am beyond blessed to have been adopted into a new family. To HOWIEEE! and Linda K., thank you for accepting me as one of your own kids and loving me without conditions. The two of you have done so much to heal my hurting heart. I love you guys. I'm also so sorry I effed up the carrot casserole with too many croutons!

To my 'sperience buddy Leeanna, thank you for being you and sharing your family with me. Your boys are the nephews I've always wanted. I'd thank you for sharing your husband too, but he's not big on the limelight, and some people might get the wrong idea.

Working through my childhood wounds has been ugly, offensive, and even scary at times. I want to express heartfelt gratitude and acknowledge those who have been around for the long haul. Much love, abundance and good health to Marie, Lori, Lisa, Val, Tracey, Gayle, and Donna. Without fail, I feel seen, heard, safe, valued, and loved in your company. I am extremely blessed to have you in my corner. When I lose my way, you remind me who I am.

Good fortune and health to my chosen brothers, Phil, Nelson, and Greg. I may not interact with you as often as I'd like, but I know in my heart, you're there. I hope you feel that too. Having that sense of safety helps me through tough times.

To the clients who have brought me into their lives like a welcome family member--thank you. Your trust in me and the work I do helps fill my heart with love and hope on the darkest days.

Recovery from growing up with abusive, neglectful, and emotionally unavailable caregivers cannot be done alone. To that end, I must acknowledge all the fellow travelers in ACA who provide the reassurance that I am neither nuts nor alone. Your authentic shares, timely check-ins, and demonstrated unconditional love have helped me navigate toward an emotionally healthier future.

Thank you, Open Door Publications and Eric Labacz Design & Illustration for all you've done to put this book together. It is an honor and a pleasure to walk this process with you. I am sending bountiful blessings to you both.

Lastly, I must thank the countless others who smiled, held a door, paid a compliment, made small talk, let me go ahead of them, bought me a coffee, or offered up another type of goodwill. Thank you for sharing unconditional love and helping to create the kind of world I really want to live in.

Kindness does matter.

About The Author

Sherri's childhood experience taught her that it's hard to hit a moving target. As such, she likes to stay active hiking, biking, playing softball, gardening, kayaking, camping, and whatever else calls to her sense of adventure in the moment. She's likely to be found playing outside, anywhere there may be animals or well-behaved children, in any kind of weather. With more lives than a cat, and similar to the Phoenix, Sherri has transformed herself many times during this lifetime. Through it all, one thing remains constant, her love for animals, nature, and spirit. Sherri currently makes her home in New Jersey with three dog-like cats, Chase, Spooky, and Boodah calling all the shots.

Sherri's work experience is as diverse as a mutt's DNA. She is a retired Information Technology professional and former elected official who now spends her "spare time" working with animals and their people. She seamlessly blends traditional training as an Animal Control Officer, Reiki Master, and Integrated Energy Therapy® Master Instructor with her spiritual gift as a non-denominational minister and Animal Communicator to give animals a voice. Sherri also officiates weddings and funerals, guides rafting trips down the Lehigh River, is available for speaking engagements, leads her county's Animal Response Team, and only God knows what else she'll add to the list before this book goes to print. People often ask her, "Is there anything you *can't* do?" The answer is always the same. "I can't cut straight with scissors."

This is Sherri's third book. Her first book, *All My Heroes Have, Fur, Fins & Feathers: An Animal Communicator's Healing Journey of Awakening* is currently in nine countries, multiple libraries including the

New Jersey Governor's Library at Drumthwacket, Amazon, and several retail outlets, including the trunk of her car.

Her second book, *Unraveled: From Sibling Abuse to Sacred Self* was released in November of 2023.

She plans to relocate to a less congested area, off the grid that has "REAL WINTERS."